The Investor's
Self-Teaching Seminars

UNDERSTANDING AND TRADING
LISTED STOCK OPTIONS

*The Investor's
Self-Teaching Seminars*

UNDERSTANDING AND TRADING LISTED STOCK OPTIONS

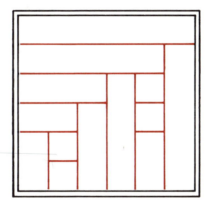

*One of a Series of Hands-On Workshops
Dedicated to the Serious Investor*

Carl F. Luft and Richard K. Sheiner

Probus Publishing Company
Chicago, Illinois

© Carl L. Luft and Richard K. Sheiner, 1988

ALL RIGHTS RESERVED. No part of this publication may be reproduced, stored in a retrieval system, or transmitted, in any form or by any means, electronic, mechanical, photocopying, recording, or otherwise, without the prior written permission of the publisher and the copyright holder.

This publication is designed to provide accurate and authoritative information in regard to the subject matter covered. It is sold with the understanding that the publisher is not engaged in rendering legal, accounting or other professional service. If legal advice or other expert assistance is required, the services of a competent professional person should be sought.

FROM A DECLARATION OF PRINCIPLES JOINTLY ADOPTED BY A COMMITTEE OF THE AMERICAN BAR ASSOCIATION AND A COMMITTEE OF PUBLISHERS.

ISBN 0-917253-90-6

Printed in the United States of America

2 3 4 5 6 7 8 9 0

Preface

This book has been written for the conservative and prudent investor. Our primary goal is to show the investor how stock options can be used to reduce risk and stabilize return. While it is true that some option strategies are extremely risky, it is also true many option strategies provide the investor with a powerful risk management tool. Thus, our secondary goal is to debunk the myth that all option investment strategies are too complex for the average investor to understand, and too risky for the average investor to undertake. Whether you are a neophyte option investor, or one who has been active in the options market for years, we feel that this book will make worthwhile reading.

In the early chapters we introduce option basics, the mechanics of the options market, and the fundamental properties of both call and put options. Later chapters introduce various option strategies which increase in complexity. The strategy chapters rely heavily on actual market examples where graphs and worksheets are used to clarify and augment the presentation. The worksheets are designed to provide the investor with ample opportunity to become familiar with all phases of the individual strategies. We feel that mastering the worksheets will give the average investor the confidence to use the various option strategies as a means of effectively managing one's risk without unduly sacrificing one's return.

We gratefully acknowledge the support of: Dr. Geoffrey Hirt, Chairman of DePaul University's Finance Department; Brother Leo Ryan, Dean of DePaul University's College of Commerce; and the DePaul University Faculty Research Council. We also wish to thank Mary Anne and Sheryl for typing portions of the manuscript, and Mr. Vincent Turcotte for his many hours of computer assistance. Finally, we want to thank all the people at Probus Publishing Company for their efforts on our behalf.

Carl F. Luft
Richard K. Sheiner

CONTENTS

PREFACE	**V**
CHAPTER ONE: INTRODUCTION TO OPTIONS	**1**
Introduction	3
Option Maturities	4
The Options Market	5
Mechanics of Options Trading	8
Some Investment Terminology	13
CHAPTER TWO: PROPERTIES OF OPTION PRICES	**17**
Option Pricing Factors	19
Components of Option Prices	19
Behavior of Call Option Prices	23
Behavior of Put Option Prices	31
Option Deltas	35
Profit Graphs for Basic Investment Position	37
Conclusion	45
CHAPTER THREE: SIMPLE CALL OPTION STRATEGIES	**47**
Purchasing Call Options Versus Purchasing Stock	49
Time Considerations	51
Purchasing a Call Option with an Existing Profit in the Stock	53
Option Deltas	53
Naked Call Writing	54

Covered Call Option Writing	55
Selling Call Options Against a Stock with an Existing Profit	66
Hedging a Short Sale	67
Conclusion	68

CHAPTER FOUR: SIMPLE PUT OPTION STRATEGIES — 69

Purchase of Put Options	71
Put Options as Insurance	75
Selling Puts	80
Conclusion	88

CHAPTER FIVE: BASIC SPREADS — 89

Definition of Spread	91
Bull Spread	91
Bean Spread	97
Time Spread	106
Illustrative Time Spread: Firestone Tire & Rubber	111
Conclusion	119
Problems	120

CHAPTER SIX: COMBINATIONS — 123

Definitions	125
Underlying Logic	126
Straddle and Strangle Purchasing Strategies	128
Straddle & Strangle Writing Strategies	132
Illustrations of the Straddle/Strangle Positions	136
Conclusion	148
Problems	149

CHAPTER SEVEN: ADVANCED OPTION STRATEGIES — 151

Buying Stock and Selling Puts Simultaneously	153
Covered Combinations	157
Hedged Covered Call Write	163
Synthetic Stock Position	168
Repair Strategy	175
Conclusion	181
Problems	181

Table of Contents

Appendix A: Bibliography	**185**
Appendix B: Glossary	**189**
Appendix C: Options Software	**197**
Appendix D: Solutions	**201**
Problem 5-1	203
Problem 5-2	205
Problem 5-3	207
Problem 5-4	209
Problem 5-5	211
Problem 5-6	213
Problem 6-1	215
Problem 6-2	217
Problem 6-3	219
Problem 6-4	221
Problem 7-1	223
Problem 7-2	224
Problem 7-3	226
Problem 7-4	228
Problem 7-5	230
Appendix E: About The Authors	**233**

Chapter One

INTRODUCTION TO OPTIONS

INTRODUCTION

An *option* is the right—rather than the obligation—to buy or sell an asset at some point in the future. A *call* option grants the right to buy the asset; a *put* option grants the right to sell it. When an option is exercised, the underlying asset changes hands at a price known as the *striking* or *exercise* price. Options can be further classified as either European or American. A *European* option can be exercised only at maturity, while an *American* option can be exercised at any time up to and including the maturity date.

Combining these concepts yields the specific definitions for call and put options. An *American call option* grants the owner the right to purchase the underlying asset for the exercise price on or before the maturity date. An *American put option* grants the owner the right to sell that asset for the exercise price on or before the maturity date. A *European call option* grants the owner the right to purchase the underlying asset for the striking price only at maturity. A *European put option* grants the holder the right to sell that asset for the striking price only at maturity.

The trading price for the option is commonly referred to as the *premium.* Thus, if one purchases a put option, one pays the premium.

If one sells, or writes, a put option, one collects the premium. All premiums are paid at the time of the sale.

It is important not to confuse the option's premium with its exercise or striking price. The exercise price is the price at which the underlying asset changes hands. For example, if an investor paid a $5 premium for a call option with a $40 striking price and then exercised the option, he or she would purchase the stock from the call writer at a price of $40 per share. In general, stocks trading at less than $200 per share have striking prices listed in $5 increments; stocks trading at values greater than $200 per share have striking prices listed in $10 increments.

OPTION MATURITIES

Virtually all exchange-traded equity options mature according to one of three standard expiration cycles:
1. January/April/July/October
2. February/May/August/November
3. March/June/September/December

Given these cycles, the longest possible maturity for an exchange-traded equity option is nine months.

In 1986, the Chicago Board Options Exchange (CBOE) initiated a program designed to take advantage of the high degree of liquidity in the shorter-maturity options for the stocks in the January expiration cycle. This program, commonly known as the *sequential option program*, attempts to satisfy the demand for shorter-maturity options by creating options with maturities of approximately 30 and 60 days. These new maturities were added to the existing five-to-nine-month maturities in the January expiration cycle. The shorter maturities provide more flexibility by guaranteeing that the investor will always have the opportunity to establish positions in one- or two-month options in these stocks. Exhibit 1-1 illustrates the sequential option expiration cycle.

Frequently the terms ''class'' and ''series'' are used when discussing options. These terms simply relate the concepts of striking price and maturity to specific options. An option *class* refers to the type of option written on a single underlying stock. Thus, exchange-

Introduction to Options 5

traded options have two separate classes—one for puts and one for calls. An option *series* is a subset of an option class. All options with the same striking price and maturity date constitute a series. Since virtually all option classes have three maturity dates, each class has at least three series of options. For example, if there are four exercise prices and three maturities, there are three series of options for that class.

Exhibit 1-1
Sequential Option Expiration Dates

Option Trading Date		Maturity Dates								
December	22	January	17	February	21	April	18	July	18	
January	19	February	21	March	21	April	18	July	18	
February	23	March	21	April	18	July	18	October	17	
March	23	April	18	May	16	July	18	October	17	
April	20	May	16	June	20	July	18	October	17	
May	18	June	20	July	18	October	17	January	16	
June	22	July	18	August	22	October	17	January	16	
July	20	August	22	September	19	October	17	January	16	
August	24	September	19	October	17	January	16	April	16	
September	21	October	17	November	21	January	16	April	16	
October	19	November	21	December	19	January	16	April	16	
November	23	December	19	January	16	April	16	July	16	

THE OPTIONS MARKET

Active trading of equity options occurs on five exchanges in the United States: the Chicago Board Options Exchange (CBOE); the American Stock Exchange (AMEX); the Philadelphia Stock Exchange (PHLX); the Pacific Stock Exchange (PSE); and the New York Stock Exchange (NYSE). All equity options traded on these exchanges are American options; there are no European exchange-traded equity options.

Exhibit 1-2 provides final option market price quotations from *The Wall Street Journal.* Since these are the quoted prices for the day's final trade, it is very unlikely that an investor would be able to transact in the options market at these prices. However, for simplicity we will use these final prices in the following explanation.

Column 1 provides the name of the underlying stock and its closing price for that particular day. Column 2 supplies the striking prices for the put and call options. Columns 3 through 5 show the final price quotes for call options maturing in December, March, and June. Columns 6 through 8 give the final prices for the put options maturing in December, March, and June.

It is important to realize that while option prices are expressed on a per-share basis, each option controls 100 shares. Thus, if one purchases a General Motors call option with a striking price of 70 and a December expiration, one will pay a premium of $200 for the right to purchase 100 shares of GM common stock, on or before the December expiration date, for a price of $70 per share. Conversely, a call option seller, or writer, will collect a $200 premium and incur the obligation to deliver 100 shares of General Motors common stock at a price of $70 per share if the call option is exercised.

Clearly not every option in Exhibit 1-2 has a final market price. For many options, the letter ''r'' or ''s'' appears in place of a price. The ''r'' indicates that although the option was available for trading, no trades took place on that day; the ''s'' means that no option of that particular series is offered for trading by the exchange.

Finally, note that the Ford options have an ''o'' following the name of the underlying stock and that the striking prices violate the general rule of $5 increments. The ''o'' alerts the investor to the fact that something unique, such as a stock split or stock dividend, is associated with the Ford options. When a stock split or dividend occurs, either the striking prices, the number of shares controlled by the option, or the number of options outstanding are adjusted. If the stock split is 1 for 1 or greater, the number of shares controlled by each option remains unchanged but the striking prices and number of outstanding options are adjusted accordingly. For example, if prior to a 2-for-1 stock split there was a series of options with a $40 striking price, after the split there would be twice as many options with a striking price of $20.

Exhibit 1-2
Listed Options Quotations (Wednesday, October 22, 1986)

Closing prices of all options. Sales unit usually is 100 shares.
Stock close is New York or American exchange final price.

Option & NY Close	Strike Price	Calls—Last Dec	Mar	Jun	Puts—Last Dec	Mar	Jun
Ford o	46 5/8	11 3/8	s	s	r	s	s
57 7/8	50	8 1/2	s	s	1/4	s	s
57 7/8	53 3/8	5 1/4	s	s	5/8	s	s
57 7/8	56 5/8	4	s	s	1 3/4	s	s
57 7/8	60	1 7/8	s	s	r	s	s
GenCp	70	r	r	r	7/8	r	r
76 1/2	75	4 3/8	r	r	r	r	r
Gen El	70	7 1/4	r	r	1/2	1 1/4	r
76 5/8	75	3 1/4	5	6 5/8	1 7/8	r	3 1/2
76 5/8	80	1	2 9/16	3 1/2	4 5/8	r	6 1/4
76 5/8	85	1/4	r	s	8 3/4	r	s
G M	65	5 1/8	6 1/2	r	13/16	2	3
69 7/8	70	2	3 1/4	4 1/8	2 3/4	4 1/4	r
69 7/8	75	9/16	1 1/2	2 3/8	6 1/2	7 1/2	r
69 7/8	80	1/4	11/16	s	r	11 1/4	s
69 7/8	85	r	1/4	s	r	r	s
Glf Wn	60	6 3/4	8 1/2	r	r	r	r
65 1/4	65	3 1/8	5 3/4	r	2 1/4	2 1/2	3 1/2
65 1/4	70	1 1/2	2 3/4	r	r	r	r
65 1/4	75	5/16	r	s	r	r	s
Heinz	35	7 1/4	r	r	r	r	r
41 7/8	40	2 3/4	4 1/4	5	3/4	1 7/16	r
41 7/8	45	5/8	1 5/8	2 3/4	r	r	r
41 7/8	50	1/8	7/8	s	r	r	s
HughTI	5	r	3	r	r	r	r
7 3/4	7 1/2	r	1 3/8	r	3/8	r	r
7 3/4	10	1/8	1/2	3/4	2 1/4	r	r
ICX Ind	20	r	r	s	1/16	r	s
25 7/8	25	1 3/8	3 1/8	r	r	r	r
25 7/8	30	3/8	1 1/8	r	r	r	r
I T T	40	r	13 1/2	s	r	r	s
53 1/8	45	8 5/8	9 1/4	9 5/8	3/16	1/2	r
53 1/8	50	4	5 3/4	6	7/8	r	r
53 1/8	55	1 3/8	3	3 3/4	2 7/8	r	r
53 1/8	60	1/2	1 1/8	s	r	r	s
K mart	40	8 1/4	r	r	r	r	1 1/8
47 3/4	45	4 1/4	5 1/2	6 1/2	1	2	2 5/8
47 3/4	50	1 5/8	3	4	r	r	r
47 3/4	55	1/2	1 1/2	s	r	r	s
Litton	70	6 1/2	r	r	r	r	r
75 1/8	75	3	r	r	2 1/4	r	r
75 1/8	80	1 1/4	r	r	r	r	r
75 1/8	85	1/2	r	s	r	10 1/2	s
75 1/8	90	1/8	s	s	r	s	s
75 1/8	95	1/16	s	s	r	s	s
Loews	60	r	r	r	5/8	r	r
65 1/2	65	2 15/16	4 3/4	r	2	r	r
65 1/2	70	r	2 7/16	r	r	6 1/8	r
MayDS	35	1 1/4	r	r	1	1 3/4	r
35 1/8	37 1/2	1/2	r	s	r	r	s
Mc Don	55	6 3/4	8 1/4	r	7/16	1 1/8	r
60 3/4	60	3	5 3/8	6 5/8	1 7/8	3	r
60 3/4	65	1 1/8	3	4 1/8	4 1/4	5 3/8	r
60 3/4	70	5/16	1 3/8	s	r	r	s
60 3/4	75	1/16	3/8	s	r	r	s
Mid SU	10	3	r	r	r	r	r
12 3/8	12 1/2	13/16	1 1/4	1 11/16	5/16	9/16	3/4
12 7/8	15	3/16	7/16	r	r	r	r
N C R	45	2 11/16	4 3/8	6	1 1/4	3	r
46	50	15/16	2 1/2	3	r	r	r
46	55	3/8	1 1/8	r	r	r	r
NorSo	75	r	r	r	r	r	2 1/4
81 1/8	80	3 1/2	r	r	1 1/2	r	r
81 1/8	85	1 1/2	r	r	r	r	r
81 1/8	90	r	1 1/2	r	r	r	r
81 1/8	95	1/8	r	s	r	r	s
81 1/8	100	1/16	s	s	r	s	s
NorTel	30	1 3/16	2 1/4	3	r	r	r
30 1/4	35	1/8	3/8	s	r	r	s
RalPur	55	13 1/4	r	r	1/16	r	r
68 5/8	60	r	r	12 1/2	r	r	r
68 5/8	65	4 3/4	6 3/4	8 1/2	1	r	r
68 5/8	70	2	3 5/8	r	3 3/8	4 1/4	r
68 5/8	75	r	1 3/4	s	7 1/8	r	s
SwAir	20	5 1/2	r	r	r	r	r
24 7/8	22 1/2	2 7/8	r	r	1/4	11/16	r
24 7/8	25	1 3/16	2 1/4	2 7/8	7/8	1 1/2	r
24 7/8	30	1/8	5/8	r	r	r	r
Syntex	50	5 1/2	7	r	1	1 3/4	r
53 7/8	55	2 1/2	4	6	2 3/4	4 1/4	5
53 7/8	60	7/8	2 3/8	3 1/2	6 3/4	6 3/4	r
53 7/8	65	5/16	1	2 3/8	11	r	r
53 7/8	70	1/4	r	s	r	r	s
Tektrn	55	r	12	r	r	3/8	r
65 3/4	60	7	r	r	5/8	r	r
65 3/4	65	3 5/8	5	6	2 1/4	3	r
Toys	25	r	r	r	3/8	3/4	r
30 1/2	30	2 1/8	r	r	1 5/8	r	r
30 1/2	35	1/2	1 1/2	r	r	r	r
U S G	35	7 1/2	7 5/8	r	1	r	r
41 3/8	40	4 3/8	5 1/2	r	2 3/4	3 1/2	4 1/4
41 3/8	45	2 1/2	3 1/4	r	5 1/2	r	r
Viacom	27 1/2	16 3/4	s	s	r	s	s
44 1/4	30	14 1/8	r	s	r	r	s
44 1/4	35	9 3/8	9 7/8	r	r	r	r
44 1/4	37 1/2	7 1/8	s	s	r	s	s
44 1/4	40	4 3/4	5 1/4	r	5/16	7/8	1 1/8
44 1/4	45	7/8	1 5/8	1 3/4	1 5/8	r	r
WalMrt	35	10	r	r	1/8	r	r
44 3/8	40	5 3/8	6 1/2	r	1/2	1	1 3/4
44 3/8	45	1 11/16	3 5/8	5	1 15/16	2 7/8	r
44 3/8	50	1/2	1 5/8	2 3/4	r	r	r
44 3/8	55	3/16	7/8	s	r	r	s
YellFr	45	r	1 1/4	r	r	r	r

Option & NY Close	Strike Price	Calls—Last Dec	Mar	Jun	Puts—Last Dec	Mar	Jun
Gillet	35	r	5 7/8	r	r	r	1 1/4
40 5/8	40	1 7/8	3	r	r	r	r
40 5/8	42 1/2	15/16	s	s	r	s	s
40 5/8	45	7/16	1 1/4	1 3/4	r	r	r
40 5/8	50	3/16	1/2	s	r	r	s
Hecla	10	r	3	r	r	r	9/16
12 1/4	12 1/2	7/8	1 1/2	1 7/8	3/4	1 3/16	1 5/8
12 1/4	15	3/16	11/16	1 1/16	r	r	r
Hercul	50	4 1/4	5 1/2	r	r	r	r
53 1/4	55	1 3/4	r	r	r	r	r
53 1/4	60	7/16	1 1/2	r	r	r	r
Kellog	45	r	r	r	7/8	r	r
48 5/8	50	1 1/2	3 1/8	r	3	3 7/8	4 1/4
L T V	5	1/16	r	s	3	r	s
PacGE	22 1/2	r	r	r	r	r	3/4
23 7/8	25	1/4	5/8	7/8	r	r	r
23 7/8	30	r	1/8	s	r	r	s
Pfizer	55	5	6 1/8	r	7/8	r	r
58 5/8	60	2	3 3/4	r	3	r	r
58 5/8	65	9/16	1 7/8	3 1/8	7	r	r
58 5/8	70	r	7/8	s	r	r	s
58 5/8	75	1/16	1/2	s	r	r	s
Ph Mor	55	r	s	s	1/16	s	s
70 5/8	60	11 1/2	r	r	1/4	3/4	r
70 5/8	65	6 3/4	7 3/4	r	7/8	r	2 5/8
70 5/8	70	2 15/16	4 3/4	r	2 1/4	3 1/2	r
70 5/8	75	1 1/16	2 11/16	3 7/8	5 1/4	r	r
70 5/8	80	3/8	1 3/8	s	r	r	s
70 5/8	85	3/16	r	s	r	r	s
PrimeC	15	r	3 1/8	r	r	r	r
17 1/2	17 1/2	1 1/8	1 3/4	r	1	r	r
17 1/2	20	3/8	15/16	1 5/8	3	3 1/8	r
17 1/2	22 1/2	1/8	5/8	r	5 1/4	r	r
SFeSP	25	5 1/4	r	r	r	r	r
30 5/8	30	1 3/8	2 1/4	r	r	r	2 5/8
30 5/8	35	1/4	3/4	1 3/8	r	r	r
Seagte	10	7 1/2	r	s	r	r	s
17 1/2	15	2 7/8	3 5/8	r	r	5/8	r
17 1/2	17 1/2	1 1/8	r	2 1/2	r	r	r
17 1/2	20	3/8	1	r	r	r	r
StdOil	40	r	r	r	3/16	9/16	r
46 5/8	45	2 3/4	4	r	1 5/8	2 1/2	3 5/8
46 5/8	50	13/16	1 3/4	r	5	5 1/2	5 1/2
46 5/8	55	1/4	r	1	r	r	r
Telex	50	10	r	s	3/16	r	s
60 5/8	55	6 1/2	7 3/4	r	5/8	1 3/4	r
60 5/8	60	2 5/8	4 1/2	r	2	r	r
60 5/8	65	1	2 3/4	4 1/8	r	r	r
60 5/8	70	3/8	s	s	r	s	s
Valero	5	3 1/4	r	r	1/16	r	r
8 3/8	7 1/2	1 1/8	1 11/16	1 7/8	1/4	5/8	r
8 3/8	10	5/16	5/8	7/8	2	r	r
8 3/8	12 1/2	1/16	s	s	r	s	s
Whitkr	30	1 5/8	r	r	r	r	r
30	35	3/16	r	r	r	r	r

Total call vol 182,355 Call open int 2,190,869
Total put vol 44,121 Put open int 567,909

r-Not Traded. s-No Option.

Option & NY Close	Strike Price	Calls—Last Dec	Mar	Jun	Puts—Last Dec	Mar	Jun
Apache	10	r	11/16	r	r	r	r
BrisMy	65	r	r	r	1/8	r	r
76 5/8	70	8 1/8	9 5/8	r	7/16	1 5/8	r
76 5/8	75	4 1/8	6 1/4	7 1/2	1 3/4	3 3/8	r
76 5/8	80	1 7/8	3 7/8	5 1/4	4 5/8	r	r
76 5/8	85	5/8	2	s	r	r	s
76 5/8	90	1/4	1 1/16	s	13 5/8	r	s
Bruns	25	5	r	r	1/4	r	r
29 5/8	30	1 3/8	2 5/8	r	r	r	r
29 5/8	35	5/16	7/8	r	r	r	r
Celan	190	r	27	s	1 5/8	r	s
209 1/2	195	r	r	s	2 1/2	5 3/4	s
209 1/2	200	14 1/2	r	r	4	r	r
209 1/2	210	8	r	r	r	11 1/2	r
209 1/2	220	5 1/4	r	r	r	r	r
209 1/2	230	2 1/8	r	s	r	r	s
Chemin	22 1/2	5 3/4	r	r	r	r	r
28 1/8	25	3 7/8	4 1/4	r	3/16	13/16	r
28 1/8	30	3/4	1 5/8	2 1/4	r	r	r
CompSc	35	2 3/8	4 1/2	r	r	r	r
Dow Ch	45	r	r	s	3/16	r	s
53 1/2	50	4 1/2	5 1/2	r	3/4	r	r
53 1/2	55	1 1/2	2 7/8	r	2 3/4	r	r
53 1/2	60	r	1 1/4	2 1/8	r	r	r
FBost	45	r	r	r	r	2	r
47 1/8	50	7/8	2 1/4	r	3 7/8	r	r
47 1/8	55	r	1 1/16	s	r	r	s
Ford	45	r	r	r	1/16	11/16	1 1/8
55 1/4	50	5 3/4	6 1/2	7 3/8	5/8	1 3/4	r
55 1/4	55	2 5/8	4	5 1/2	2 5/8	4 1/4	5 1/4
55 1/4	60	15/16	2	3	r	r	r
55 1/4	65	5/16	1	s	r	r	s
Ford o	53 3/8	3	s	s	1 15/16	s	s
GenCp	70	8	r	r	r	r	r
76 1/4	75	4 1/2	r	r	r	r	r
76 1/4	80	2	r	5 1/2	5 3/4	6 1/4	r
Gen El	65	11 1/2	r	r	1/8	r	r
76 5/8	70	7	r	9 1/8	9/16	1 7/16	r
76 5/8	75	3 1/8	4 5/8	r	2	3 1/8	r
76 5/8	80	1	2 1/2	r	r	r	r
76 5/8	85	1/4	1 1/4	s	r	r	s
G M	65	3 3/4	4 3/4	5 1/2	1 3/16	2 1/2	3 5/8
68 7/8	70	1 5/16	2 1/2	3 1/2	3 7/8	5 1/4	r
68 7/8	75	5/16	1	1 5/8	8	r	r
68 7/8	80	1/8	1/2	s	r	r	s
68 7/8	85	1/4	r	s	r	r	s
Glf Wn	60	6 3/8	7 1/2	r	1	1 3/4	r
65	65	3 1/4	4 7/8	r	2 3/4	r	r
65	70	1 3/8	r	s	r	r	s
65	75	3/8	r	s	r	r	s
Heinz	40	3	4 1/4	r	7/8	r	r
42 1/4	45	5/8	1 1/2	r	r	r	r
HughTI	5	2 1/2	3 1/4	r	r	r	r
7 3/4	7 1/2	1	1 1/8	r	1/2	r	r
7 3/4	10	1/4	3/4	1	2 3/4	r	r
7 3/4	12 1/2	1/16	1/8	s	r	r	s
ICX Ind	25	1 1/2	r	r	r	r	r
25 5/8	30	r	1	1 1/8	r	r	r
25 5/8	35	1/16	r	s	r	r	s
I T T	45	8 1/2	r	r	5/16	7/8	r
52 1/2	50	3 5/8	5 1/4	r	1 1/8	2	r
52 1/2	55	1 1/4	2 3/4	r	r	r	r
52 1/2	60	7/16	1 3/8	s	r	r	s
K mart	45	3 1/4	4 1/2	r	1 1/4	2 5/8	3
46 5/8	50	1 3/16	2 3/4	3 3/4	4 1/8	5 1/4	r
46 5/8	55	3/8	1 3/8	s	r	r	s
46 5/8	60	1/8	r	s	r	r	s
Litton	70	r	r	r	3/4	r	r
74 3/4	75	3 1/8	r	r	r	r	r
74 3/4	80	1 1/4	3 3/8	5 3/8	6	r	r
74 3/4	85	1/2	1 1/2	s	r	r	s
Loews	65	2 5/8	r	r	r	r	4
MayDS	37 1/2	3	r	s	r	r	s
34 3/4	35	1 3/16	r	r	r	r	r
34 3/4	37 1/2	9/16	r	s	r	r	s
34 3/4	40	r	1/2	11/16	r	r	r
Mc Don	55	4 5/8	6 5/8	r	7/8	1 3/4	2 1/2
58 1/8	60	1 7/8	3 7/8	r	3 1/8	r	r
58 1/8	65	11/16	2	r	6 3/4	r	r
58 1/8	70	r	1 1/16	s	r	r	s
Mid SU	12 1/2	11/16	1 1/16	r	7/16	11/16	7/8
12 1/2	15	1/8	3/8	9/16	2 1/2	2 1/2	r
N C R	40	5 7/8	r	r	9/16	r	r
45	45	2 1/2	r	r	2 1/8	3 3/4	r
45	50	13/16	2 5/8	3 3/4	5 3/8	r	r
45	55	5/16	7/8	r	r	r	r
45	60	3/16	r	s	r	r	s
NorSo	80	5 1/4	r	r	r	r	r
84	85	2 1/4	r	r	3 5/8	r	r
84	90	9/16	2	r	r	r	r
NorTel	30	13/16	1 3/4	r	r	1 7/8	r
RalPur	60	r	r	r	1/4	1 1/8	r
67 7/8	65	r	5 3/4	r	1 1/2	2 1/2	r
67 7/8	70	1 1/2	r	r	4 3/8	r	r
67 7/8	75	r	1 3/4	s	r	r	s
SwAir	20	5	r	r	r	r	r
25	22 1/2	2 7/8	3 3/4	r	1/4	r	r
25	25	1 1/4	1 7/8	2 1/2	7/8	r	r
25	30	r	r	9/16	r	r	r
Syntex	50	4 1/2	6 5/8	r	1 1/4	2	r
53 3/8	55	2 1/4	3 3/4	r	2 7/8	4 1/4	r
53 3/8	60	13/16	2 1/8	3 1/2	r	r	r
53 3/8	65	3/8	1	r	r	r	r
53 3/8	70	3/16	r	s	r	r	s
53 3/8	75	1/8	3/8	s	r	r	s

MECHANICS OF OPTIONS TRADING

THE CLEARING PROCESS So far, nothing specific has been said about trading exchange-listed options. To grasp the market mechanics, one must understand how the Options Clearing Corporation (OCC) relates to option market participants. The OCC guarantees the performance of all equity option contracts that are traded on all of the federally designated exchanges. Since there must be a buyer for each option sold, all option purchases and sales must match at the end of the day. The OCC facilitates this daily matching and, in the process, becomes the opposite party to all trades. The OCC's ability to become the writer for every buyer and the buyer for every writer means that investors need not worry about contract performance or locating someone to take an offsetting position. Thus, individual investors can easily create or liquidate positions unilaterally. While the OCC is the ultimate guarantor of the option contract, the investor has virtually no direct contact with it; rather, it is the investor's brokerage house that must clear all trades through a member of the OCC. Exhibit 1-3 illustrates the clearing process structure.

THE ORDER PROCESS On the floor of the Chicago Board Options Exchange are three types of brokers who can execute trades: floor brokers, market makers, and order book officials. *Floor brokers* usually are salaried employees of brokerage houses and execute orders for public customers. *Market makers* trade for their own accounts and are prohibited from executing orders on behalf of public customers. *Order book officials* are employees of the Chicago Board Options Exchange and maintain a book of unfilled limit orders. Bid and ask price information for the limit orders that are closest to the current market quote is constantly made available by the order book official to the floor brokers and market makers. If there appears to be little chance of a limit order being executed, a floor broker may elect to place the order with the order book official. Once in the book, the exchange guarantees that when the market reaches the order's limit, the order will be executed based on its price and time of entry into the book.

Introduction to Options

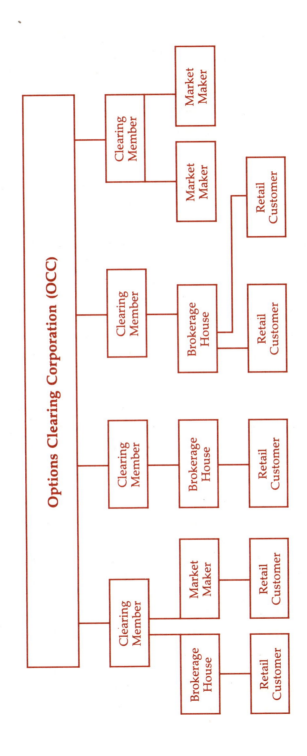

Exhibit 1-3
Clearing Process Structure

When an investor places an option order with a brokerage house, certain information is required. The investor must specify whether a put or a call is to be bought or sold; the name of the underlying stock; the striking price; the expiration month; the type of order (market or limit); and whether the order is an opening or closing transaction.

Basically there are two types of orders: market and limit. A *market order* is an order to either buy or sell the option at the current market price, and it is executed immediately. A *limit order* is an order to buy or sell an option at a specified or better price and is executed only if the market reaches the specified limit. However, if the market moves rapidly through the limit, it may not be possible to transact at the designated price. Unless specified otherwise, all orders are *day orders,* i.e., good until the end of the trading day. However, the investor can issue instructions that the order remain in effect until cancelled—hence the name *good till cancelled (GTC)*. If an order is used to establish an initial position that increases the number of outstanding options, or open interest, in the market, it is classified as an *opening transaction*. Conversely, an order that cancels an existing position and reduces the number of outstanding options is known as a *closing transaction*.

After the order has been placed with the brokerage house, it is transmitted to the exchange by telephone. A phone clerk then time stamps the order and gives it to a runner. The runner delivers the order to the floor broker whom the brokerage house uses for trading. If the order is a market order, it will be executed immediately at the prevailing market price. The floor broker may transact with another floor broker, a market maker, or the order book official. Once the trade has been completed, the two brokers verify the transaction. Then a copy of the verification is given to the runner, who returns it to the phone clerk. The phone clerk time stamps the order and notifies the brokerage house. The brokerage house then notifies the investor regarding the terms of the trade and its completion. The typical time period between order placement and confirmation by the brokerage house is 10 minutes. At this point, full payment for the option is due on the next business day, and the investor can expect written confirmation of the order from the brokerage house within five days. Exhibit 1-4 provides a schematic of the order process.

Introduction to Options

**Exhibit 1-4
Order Process**

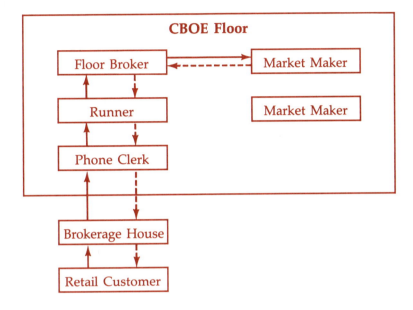

Indicates the order information flow originating with the retail customer.

Indicates the trade confirmation information flow ending with the retail customer.

THE EXERCISE PROCESS When an option holder decides to exercise, the brokerage house is notified first. The brokerage house then uses its clearing member to inform the OCC. The OCC in turn randomly selects and notifies a clearing member, who has an open-write position, of the assignment. If call options are being exercised, the assigned clearing member must deliver 100 shares of the underlying stock at the striking price for each option exercised to the clearing member who is exercising the calls. For put options, the assigned clearing member must accept 100 shares of the underlying stock at the striking price for each option being exercised by the clearing member who initiated the process. Upon delivering shares to satisfy the call option's exercise, or receiving shares to satisfy the put option's exercise, the assigned clearing member either delivers shares to, or receives shares from, a customer who is short a put or a call.

An investor may choose to exercise an equity option at any point during its life. However, notification of exercise must be given prior to 4:30 p.m. Central Time on the third Friday of the option's expiration month. The reason for this is twofold. First, the option's last trading day is the third Friday of the expiration month because the option expires on the following day, Saturday, at 10:59 a.m. Central Time. Second, the exchanges have imposed a notification deadline of 4:30 p.m. Central Time on the option's last trading day. This deadline is only 90 minutes after options trading ceases on all exchanges at 3:00 p.m. Central Time.

LIMITS AND MARGIN REQUIREMENTS In addition to the trading and notification deadlines, the investor should be aware of position limits, exercise limits, and general margin requirements. The position and exercise limits are imposed to prevent manipulation of the option market. Margins are required to help insure contract performance.

A *position limit* prohibits an investor, or group of investors, from owning or writing more than a specified number of options constituting the same side of the market. One is considered to be on the same side of the market if one simultaneously writes calls and buys puts, or vice versa. In the first situation, shares will be delivered if exercise of both the puts and the calls occurs. In the second, shares will be accumulated from the exercise of both puts and calls. *Exercise limits* usually match position limits and can range from 2,000 to 8,000 contracts, depending on the stock's price and trading volume. Specific position and exercise limits can be obtained from the exchange on which the option is traded.

Margin requirements for options are subject to change and wide variation among brokerage houses. However, option buyers generally must pay the full amount within one day of purchase. The reason is that the option itself is a levered instrument. For the price of an equity option, the investor can control 100 shares of the underlying stock. Option writers who do not own the underlying stock are required to deposit an amount equal to 15 percent of the stock's current market value plus the entire call or put premium received. This margin may be posted in Treasury bills or cash. For writers who own the underlying shares, the margins are much lower and can be posted in cash, Treasury bills, or shares of stock. Usually it is unwise to post a cash margin because, unlike with Treasury bills, one must forgo interest.

SOME INVESTMENT TERMINOLOGY

The following chapters use certain terms having unique meanings within the investment industry to describe various option strategies. To achieve the greatest possible understanding of these strategies, one must be familiar with these terms.

MARKET FORECASTS The best starting point is the investor's outlook for market performance. An investor who is optimistic about the markets in general is considered *bullish*. A pessimistic investor is said to be *bearish*. An invester who expects markets to exhibit little movement either way is considered *neutral*. Bullish investors anticipate rising markets, bearish investors expect falling markets, and neutral investors presume that markets will be flat.

Investors formulate their market forecasts in a variety of ways. The two most common methods of evaluating market conditions are fundamental analysis and technical analysis.

An investor who relies on *fundamental analysis* uses the relationships exhibited by basic economic, industry, and individual firm variables to assess the condition of financial markets, specific industries, or individual firms. For example, if an investor thinks that interest rates will increase because of rising inflation and that a recession is likely, he or she will probably be bearish on both the stock and bond markets.

An investor uses *technical analysis* when relying on market-related data such as past prices, trading volume, number of advancing shares, or short-selling activity to form an opinion about the markets in general, a specific industry, or a particular firm. The technician's goal is to first discern the nature of price trends and then take positions that will allow him or her to profit from them. For example, suppose an investor has found a stock that appears to have an upward price trend. Based on this pattern, the investor may turn bullish and purchase the stock.

The basic difference between technical and fundamental analysis is that pure technical analysis does not consider basic economic relationships; it relies solely on internal market data. On the other hand, fundamental analysis rejects isolated market data and focuses on the relationship of the basic underlying factors that determine a security's value.

SHORT SELLING Earlier in this chapter, we described investors as being either option sellers or option buyers. However, it is less cumbersome—and more consistent with industry practice—to characterize an investor who has purchased an asset as being *long* the asset and the seller of the asset as being *short* the asset. Thus, an investor who is bullish and has purchased stock is long the stock, and one who has purchased an option is long the option. Conversely, an option writer is considered short the option. The short stock position is quite complex and requires a detailed explanation.

Being *short stock* implies that the investor has sold stock. More precisely, the short position has been attained through a short sale. Three parties are needed for a short sale to occur: the stock's short seller, the stock's purchaser, and a lender of the shares to be sold short. The share lender is required because the short seller does not own the stock being sold.

The process begins with a bearish investor who believes that the stock's price is going to drop. In order to capture as much of the stock's current value as possible, the investor short sells shares of the stock to the purchaser. At this point, the seller has five business days in which to deliver the shares and the stock purchaser five business days to pay for them. To satisfy the delivery requirement, the short seller borrows shares from the share lender—usually a brokerage house—and delivers them to the share buyer. From this point on, the share buyer is of no further consequence—indeed, he or she probably neither knows nor cares that the shares were purchased from a short seller.

During the period over which the shares have been lent, the share lender demands compensation from the short seller in the form of interest. Further, the short seller is required to pay all dividends to which the share lender is entitled. Finally, the share lender requires the short seller to deposit a portion of the sale proceeds. Thus, the short seller does not have full use of the sale proceeds and must pay the share lender interest as well.

If the stock drops as anticipated, the short seller will purchase enough shares in the market to close out the short position by replenishing the share lender's portfolio. The short seller can profit by purchasing stock at a market price that is lower than the sale price and low enough to cover all costs associated with the short-sale transaction. If the stock rises, the short seller will lose. The share lender will demand that the shares be replenished, and the short seller will have no choice but to purchase the stock at a market price higher than the sale price. If the short seller cannot fund the stock purchase, the share lender has a legal right to demand the short seller to liquidate positions in other assets, such as stocks and bonds, in order to cover the short position. Obviously short selling is a very risky proposition, since the potential for unlimited loss is extremely high.

LEVERAGE   The term *leverage* means that an investor can assume a position in a security by investing less than the full amount of the security's face value. Since a single option controls 100 shares of stock and enables the investor to benefit from price changes in the underlying security at a fraction of the security's cost, options are levered instruments. When an investor creates a highly levered position, there is great potential for profit. However, as with short selling, there is also the risk of a large loss. It is true that leverage magnifies an investor's return, but it is equally true that leverage intensifies losses.

CAPITAL GAINS AND LOSSES   The concepts of gains and losses must be understood within the context of capital assets, that is, equities and their associated options. *Capital gains* are the gains resulting from changing values of stock and options; *capital losses* are any losses incurred due to changing stock and option values. Precise computation of capital gains and losses depends on the asset's cost basis. In general, the cost basis of any asset is the asset's price plus all transaction costs that are paid at the time of its purchase. This cost basis is used to determine the investor's capital gain or loss when the position is liquidated.

CONCLUSION

It is appropriate to conclude this chapter with two caveats. First, one should be aware that brokerage commissions fluctuate widely within the investment industry. For this reason, we will ignore commissions throughout the remainder of this book in both text and examples. Second, an investor should consult a competent tax counselor before undertaking any option strategy.

Chapter
Two

PROPERTIES OF OPTION PRICES

OPTION PRICING FACTORS

Recall that a *stock option* is the right to buy or sell shares of stock on or before a specific date for a specified price known as the *exercise* or *striking price.* Given this definition, it follows that option prices are intimately related to:

1. The underlying stock's price
2. The underlying stock's dividends
3. The volatility of the underlying stock's price changes
4. The time remaining to the option's maturity
5. The option's exercise price
6. Interest rates

This chapter focuses on the relationships of option prices to these six underlying factors.

COMPONENTS OF OPTION PRICES

Before one can fully comprehend the behavior of option prices, it is necessary to understand the concepts of intrinsic value, in-the-money options, at-the-money options, out-of-the-money options, and parity. These terms are most easily explained by using an approach that moves backward from an option's maturity to the present time.

INTRINSIC VALUE Recall that a call option grants the owner the right—rather than the obligation— to buy shares of the underlying stock. Thus, at maturity a call option will be worth either nothing or the difference between the current price of the underlying stock and the option's exercise price. This difference is known as the call option's *intrinsic value.* No other values are possible, since there is no time remaining in the call option's life. If the stock price is less than the exercise price, a rational investor who owns the call option will not exercise it because the underlying stock can be purchased in the open market at a price lower than the option's exercise price. Thus, the right to call shares at the exercise price is worthless, and the call option has no intrinsic value. However, if the underlying stock's price is greater than the option's exercise price, the call option has intrinsic value and its owner can exercise the option and purchase shares of the underlying stock for the exercise price. At this point, the investor can keep the shares or sell them for their current market price, which is greater than the exercise price. In this case, the right to call shares for the exercise price is worth the difference between the price of the underlying stock and the option's exercise price, or its intrinsic value.

It is obvious that the call option's intrinsic value is determined by the relationship between the price of the underlying stock and the option's exercise price. If the price of the underlying stock is greater than the option's exercise price, the option has intrinsic value and is said to be *in-the-money.* If the stock's price is less than or equal to the option's exercise price, the option has zero intrinsic value. An option is *at-the-money* when the stock price equals its exercise price and *out-of-the-money* when the stock price is less than this price. For example, if Disney common stock is trading at a price of 40, the Disney call options that have a striking price of 35 are 5 points in-the-money, or 40-35; those with a striking price of 40 are at-the-money; and those with a striking price of 45 are 5 points out-of-the-money, or 40-45.

The same logic used to determine a call option's price at maturity can be used in the case of a put option. However, it is important to remember that the put option grants the owner, or puchaser, the right to sell shares of the underlying stock at the exercise price, while the call option grants the owner the right to buy shares of the under-

Properties of Option Prices

lying stock at the exercise price. This fundamental distinction between put and call options translates into a difference in their intrinsic values.

Like the call option, the put option will have one of two values at maturity: zero or the difference between the exercise price and the underlying stock's price. Since the put option grants the owner the right to sell shares at the exercise price, it will have a positive value at maturity if the price of the underlying stock is less than the option's exercise price. In this case, the owner will exercise the put option by delivering shares of the underlying stock in exchange for the exercise price, which is greater than the stock's current market price. The right to sell stock at the exercise price is worth the difference between that price and the stock's current market price— that is, the put option's intrinsic value. If the stock price is greater than the exercise price at maturity, the put option is worthless and has no intrinsic value, since a rational investor will not exercise it and sell shares at an exercise price lower than the stock's current market price.

It is clear that the put option's intrinsic value, like the call option's, is determined by the relationship between the put option's exercise price and the market price of the underlying stock. A put option has a positive intrinsic value, and is considered to be in-the-money, when the underlying stock's price is less than the exercise price. When the price of the underlying stock is greater than the put option's exercise price, the option has no intrinsic value and is considered out-of-the-money. If the underlying stock's price equals the put option's exercise price, the option is at-the-money and has no intrinsic value. These distinctions can also be illustrated with the Disney example. If Disney common stock is trading at 40, the Disney put options that have a striking price of 45 are 5 points in-the-money, or 45-40; those with a striking price of 40 are at-the-money; and those with a striking price of 35 are 5 points out-of-the-money, or 35-40.

Note that if a put option and a call option are written on the same stock and have identical exercise prices, both will be at-the-money at the same time. Further, when the call option is in-the-money, the put option is out-of-the-money, and vice versa. These relationships are due to the fundamental difference in the options' nature and changes in the underlying stock's price. The option's exercise price does not change; it is fixed until the option contracts mature. These relationships are summarized in Exhibit 2-1.

Exhibit 2-1
Option Intrinsic Values

Call option intrinsic value = stock price − strike price
Put option intrinsic value = strike price − stock price

	Call Option	**Put Option**
Stock price > strike price	In-the-money	Out-of-the-money
Stock price = strike price	At-the-money	At-the-money
Stock price < strike price	Out-of-the-money	In-the-money

TIME PREMIUM Up to this point, we have focused on option prices at maturity. Now we will turn to option prices prior to maturity.

It is common industry practice to use the terms *premium* and *price* interchangeably. From the previous discussion, it follows that at the option's maturity its premium is either zero or its intrinsic value. Thus, at maturity the option's price, or premium, has only one component: its intrinsic value. Prior to maturity, the option's premium will have a second component known as a *time premium*. Consequently, the premium may be expressed as:

Option Premium = Intrinsic Value + Time Premium

This general representation of an option premium applies to both put and call options. It is important to understand that the time premium is a *component* of the option's premium and not equivalent to it. When industry jargon is used in discussing options, "time premium" is usually made explicit. The term "premium" therefore should be interpreted as the option's price.

PARITY An option that is trading for its intrinsic value is said to be trading at *parity*. An option that is trading at parity has no time premium. At maturity, options will trade for either zero or parity.

Prior to maturity, only deep-in-the-money options have a chance of trading at parity.

Option premiums are sometimes quoted with respect to parity. For example, the price of a deep-in-the-money call option with a premium of 21, an exercise price of 15, and an underlying stock price of 35 may be stated as being 1 point above its parity value of 20, 35-15.

BEHAVIOR OF CALL OPTION PRICES

RELATIONSHIP TO UNDERLYING STOCK PRICE The relationship between a call option's price and the price of the underlying stock is straightforward. The relationship is positive and is based on the fact that a position in a call option is a levered position in the underlying stock. If the stock price rises, the value of the right to purchase shares at the exercise price also increases. Conversely, if the stock price drops, the value of the right to purchase the option's underlying shares diminishes.

This positive relationship can prove quite useful if one feels bullish about a stock and wants to maximize the percentage gain in the near term. For example, suppose an investor feels that Sears stock is going to rise by about 5 points prior to the next dividend payment date in three months. If Sears is currently selling for 40 and the 90-day at-the-money calls—i.e., call options with a striking price of 40—are trading at 2, the investor can participate in the price movement of 100 shares of Sears stock by purchasing a 90-day call option for a price of $200. If Sears stock rises 5 points over the next 60 days, the investor's Sears call options with an exercise price of 40 and a 30-day maturity will be worth approximately 5¼ points, or $525.

If the investor decides to close the option position and take the profits, the percentage gain will be computed as:

$$\text{Percentage Gain} = \frac{\$525 - \$200}{\$200}$$

$$= 162\%$$

$$\text{Annualized Percentage Gain} = 162\% \times \frac{12 \text{ months}}{2 \text{ months}}$$

$$= 975\%$$

Such a percentage gain will be much greater than that enjoyed by an investor who has purchased 100 shares of Sears stock at 40 and then liquiated the position at 45. The stock investor's percentage gain will be computed as:

$$\text{Percentage Gain} = \frac{\$4{,}500 - \$4{,}000}{\$4{,}000}$$
$$= 12.5\%$$

$$\text{Annualized Percentage Gain} = 12.5\% \times \frac{12 \text{ months}}{2 \text{ months}}$$
$$= 75\%$$

It must be emphasized that the option investor's extremely large percentage gain is much riskier than the stock investor's. The reason for the great disparity in the riskiness of the positions is that the option has a limited life and will mature in the near future, but the stock has an infinite life and will exist long after the option matures.

To see how the riskiness of these positions differs, assume that both investors have $4,000 to invest in Sears stock. Again assume that Sears stock is selling for $40 and 90-day at-the-money call options are selling for 2. The stock investor's $4,000 results in a long position in 100 shares of Sears stock—$4,000/$40—which have an unlimited life. The option investor's $4,000 produces a long position in 20 at-the-money call options—$4,000/$200—which will expire in 90 days. Now suppose that over the next 90 days the price of Sears stock drops to $37. Both investors will suffer a loss, but the option investor's loss will be much greater than the stock investor's. After 90 days, the value of the stock position will be $3,700 ($37 × 100 shares) and the value of the option position will be zero. The option investor's position will have expired worthless, since the call options were out-of-the-money at expiration. The percentage gains and losses for each position are:

$$\text{Stock Position Percentage Loss} = \frac{\$3,700 - \$4,000}{\$4,000}$$

$$= -7.5\%$$

$$\text{Stock Position Annualized Loss} = \frac{-7.5\% \times 12 \text{ months}}{3 \text{ months}}$$

$$= 30\%$$

$$\text{Option Position Percentage Loss} = \frac{\$0 - \$4,000}{\$4,000}$$

$$= -100\%$$

$$\text{Option Position Annualized Loss} = \frac{-100\% \times 12 \text{ months}}{3 \text{ months}}$$

$$= -400\%$$

This example clearly demonstrates that there is a trade-off between the risk and return of investment alternatives. Prior to investing, one should always be fully aware of the position's riskiness as well as its potential return.

RELATIONSHIP TO CASH DIVIDENDS An inverse relationship exists between the call option's price and the underlying stock's dividends. This concept is easy to grasp given the prior discussion about the relationship between the call option's price and the stock's price. It is common knowledge that on the ex-dividend date, the value of the stock declines by the amount of the dividend at the opening trade. Thus, it follows that the call option's price should drop, since the stock's price is declining by the amount of the dividend.

Usually it is unwise for a call option owner to exercise the option before maturity, because one forfeits the option's potential gain associated with an increase in the price of the underlying stock. However, the inverse relationship between the call option price and the cash dividend is important since it can create circumstances that optimize early exercise of the call option. For example, if the call option is deep-in-the-money just prior to the stock's ex-dividend date, the owner very likely will exercise the option in order to capture the dividend. The higher the dividend's value, the greater the chance of exercise. This means that the call option writer will be assigned the obligation to deliver shares at the exercise price. If the writer wishes to avoid assignment, the open short position in the call option must be covered by purchasing an identical call option before the end of the day's trading.

RELATIONSHIP TO STOCK PRICE VOLATILITY The third key factor that determines a call option's price is the *volatility* of the price changes in the underlying stock. The greater the volatility of the underlying stock, the greater the chance that the call option will gain intrinsic value and go deep-in-the-money. If the call option is in-the-money at expiration, it will be profitable for the owner to exercise it.

This positive relationship between the call option's price and the underlying stock's price volatility should not be confused with the positive relationship between the stock price and the call option price. It is possible for a stock's price to increase and its volatility to shrink. For example, if a firm's stock is trading at $25 and it is announced that the firm has agreed to be taken over at $40 per share and the deal will be consummated in 30 days, the share price will immediately jump to $40 and remain there for the next 30 days. Since there is no reason for the stock to trade at any value less than $40, its volatility will now be virtually zero. In this example, the firm's call options with exercise prices of less than $40 will go in-the-money immediately and be priced according to their intrinsic values. However, over the next 30 days there will be very little price change in the option, since the stock's price will be fixed at $40 and the volatility will have shrunk to zero.

This positive relationship between stock price volatility and call option prices implies that in general, the greater the stock price volatility, the higher the call option's price. This relationship also suggests why riskier, more price-volatile stocks tend to have call option prices that are less stable than call option prices for more conservative stocks. Once again, the greater the stock's price volatility, the greater the risk. Thus, investors will require relatively greater returns before they will commit their funds to either the option or the underlying stock.

It should be mentioned that the stock price volatility is the only pricing factor that is not directly observable. Since the call option price is very sensitive to changes in the stock's price volatility, it is crucial that accurate volatility estimates be obtained if one is attempting to speculate in mispriced options. However, since this book's primary objective is to provide guidance for the conservative investor, volatility estimating techniques will not be discussed.

RELATIONSHIP TO TIME TO MATURITY The relationship between call option prices and the fourth option pricing factor—time—is positive. Call options written on the same underlying stock that have identical striking prices but varying maturities will have different prices. Longer-term call options will have higher prices than shorter-term ones. The higher prices for the longer-term options reflect their greater time premium values and should be expected because these options have more time to gain intrinsic value than do their shorter-term counterparts.

Since call options are *wasting* or *depleting assets,* the time premium will decay as time passes and the options approach maturity. The closer a call option is to maturity, the more rapid will be the time premium's decay. This accelerating-decay process indicates that the market believes there is little chance of the call options gaining intrinsic value in the short time remaining until expiration. A diagram of the time premium's decay is given in Exhibit 2-2.

Exhibit 2-2 clearly shows that a call option is a depleting asset and highlights the fact that the time premium decay is quite small until about six weeks before expiration. Indeed, stock price volatility is much more important than time premium decay until around 45 days from expiration. After that, the importance of the call option's remaining time until expiration increases dramatically and has a much greater effect on the option's price than before.

One subtlety in the relationship between a call option's price and time to maturity is the fact that the time premium is greatest for at-the-money call options. Call options that are either deep-in-the-money or deep-out-of-the-money have very small time premiums. The reason large time premiums occur for at-the-money call options and small time premiums occur for far-from-the-money options is that a call option's time premium expresses the market's estimate of the likelihood that the option will either gain or lose intrinsic value. The deep-out-of-the-money call options' small time premiums indi-

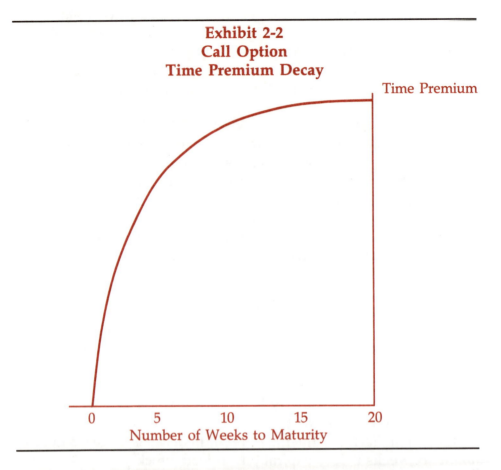

cate that there is little chance that the underlying stock's price will experience a large enough price increase to give the options positive intrinsic value before expiration. The small time premiums for the deep-in-the-money call options show that there is little chance that the price of the underlying stock will fall far enough to give the options zero intrinsic value before expiration. Finally, the large time premiums for the at-the-money call options, which have a relatively long time remaining to expiration, reflect the high probability that the underlying stock will rise sufficiently to allow the options to gain intrinsic value. However, if the price of the underlying stock does not change, these time premiums will decay rapidly as expiration approaches. Exhibit 2-3 uses IBM stock and call option prices to illustrate how time premium values differ.

Exhibit 2-3
Call Option Price Quotations
WSJ, 9/26/86

	Option and N.Y. Close	Striking Price	Calls—Last		
			Oct.	Nov.	Jan.
IBM	135½	130	6⅝	8	10
	135½	135	3¼	4¾	7
	135½	140	1¼	2¾	4⅞
	135½	145	½	1¼	2¹⁵⁄₁₆

The first thing to note about Exhibit 2-3 is that the prices of the IBM 135 call options increase with maturity. Since these options have an intrinsic value of ½ point (135½ − 135), the higher prices for the November and January options occur because of greater time values for the farther-term options: 4¼ (4¾ − ½) for the November 135 call options and 6½ (7 − ½) for the January 135 calls. By reading down the October maturity column, it is easy to see how the time premium shrinks for the far-from-the-money options. Specifically, the October 130 call option's price of 6⅝ is composed of 5½ points of intrinsic value (135½ − 130) and only 1⅛ points of time premium (6⅝ − 5½), while the October 135 call option's price of 3¼ has ½ point of intrinsic value (135½ − 130) but 2¾ points of time premium (3¼ − ½). Finally, note that the deep-out-of-the-money October 145 call option has no intrinsic value and only ½ point of time premium.

RELATIONSHIP TO EXERCISE PRICE   The relationship between the call option's price and the fifth pricing factor—the exercise price—is negative. Call options written on the same stock and with identical maturities will have different values because of their striking prices. The deep-out-of-the-money call options have high striking prices and low premiums, because they have relatively lower intrinsic values. Conversely, as call options go in-the-money they become more expensive. The call options with relatively low striking prices will have high intrinsic values that will be reflected in relatively higher option prices. This inverse relationship between the call option's price and the exercise price is readily apparent in Exhibit 2-3. Note that as one moves down the table, the exercise prices increase but the call option prices decrease.

RELATIONSHIP TO INTEREST RATES   The final relationship to be discussed is the positive correlation between call option prices and unanticipated changes in interest rates. Simply stated, higher interest rates generally lead to higher call option prices, while lower interest rates result in lower call option prices. This positive relationship means that call option prices will move in the same direction as an unanticipated move in the interest rate if the underlying stock price does not change. The logic behind this relationship becomes clear if one recognizes that the call option buyer's levered position in the stock is being financed by a loan from the call option writer. The call option writer is postponing the benefits associated with converting the stock to cash by providing the buyer with the opportunity to take a levered position in the underlying stock. High interest rates translate into a high opportunity cost for the call option writer. Thus, the writer will demand a higher call option premium as compensation for the inability to take full advantage of the higher interest rates.

The concept of *present value* provides an alternative explanation for the positive relationship between call option prices and changing interest rates. If a call option is exercised at maturity, 100 shares of the underlying stock will be purchased for an amount equal to the option's exercise price. At any time prior to maturity, the call option's premium will reflect the present value of the option's exercise price, where the present value is computed by discounting the exercise price from the option's maturity date to the present time at the risk-free interest rate. Therefore, higher interest rates result in lower present values for the exercise price and greater call option intrinsic values. Lower interest rates have the opposite effect: higher present values for the exercise price and lower call option intrinsic values. It must be emphasized that one should not expect higher call option prices when interest rates increase if the price of the underlying stock drops. This relationship is predictable only if the stock price remains unchanged.

BEHAVIOR OF PUT OPTION PRICES

In this section, we turn to the behavior of put option prices with respect to the same basic pricing factors.

Recall that a put option grants the owner the right to sell shares of the underlying stock for the exercise price on or before the option's expiration date. Although the put option differs fundamentally from the call option, the same pricing factors that determine the call option's price affect the put option's price. Also, as with call options, the intrinsic value concept provides the key to understanding the behavior of put option prices.

RELATIONSHIP TO UNDERLYING STOCK PRICE   The relationship between the put option's price and the underlying stock's price is negative—exactly opposite to the call option. Recall that since a put option grants the right to sell shares at the exercise price, this privilege becomes less valuable to the owner as the stock price rises, hence the option loses intrinsic value; if the price of the underlying stock declines, the put option gains intrinsic value.

A major consequence of this inverse relationship is that there is an upper limit on the put option's value that is equal to the option's exercise price. This maximum value exists because the stock's price can never be less than zero. Thus, if the stock's value falls to zero, the put option's intrinsic value will equal the exercise price minus the stock's current price, namely the exercise price. In the case of the call option, on the other hand, there is no theoretical upper limit on the option's value because there is no such limit on the price of the stock and, therefore, none on the option's intrinsic value.

Given the inverse relationship between the underlying stock price and the put option's price, investors obviously can use put options to profit from falling stock prices. For example, suppose an investor is bearish and predicts a drop in the price of Bethlehem Steel stock within the next three months. By simply purchasing a 6-month at-the-money put option on Bethlehem stock, the investor can benefit from any price decline that occurs. However, if the stock price fails to drop, or even rises, during the put option's life, the investor's maximum loss will be the price paid for the put option, that is, the put option's premium.

RELATIONSHIP TO CASH DIVIDENDS The relationship between the put option's price and the underlying stock's cash dividends is positive. This is not surprising, since the stock price will decline just prior to a dividend payment, which causes the put option to gain intrinsic value. This implies that the put option holder will not exercise prior to the ex-dividend date since it would be foolish to sacrifice the resulting stock price decline and increase in intrinsic value. Further, if two stocks are identical in all respects except their cash dividend payments, the stock with the larger dividend will have a higher put option price because it will experience a greater share price decline than the stock with the lower dividend.

RELATIONSHIP TO STOCK PRICE VOLATILITY A positive relationship exists between the third option pricing factor, stock price volatility, and the price of a put option. Note that this relationship is similar to that between a call option's price and the underlying stock's price volatility. Indeed, the same logic prevails for both puts and calls: The greater the underlying stock's price volatility, the greater the chance that the option will gain intrinsic value and be profitable for the owner to exercise.

Clearly, large stock price declines will add intrinsic value to put option positions. Thus, stocks with high volatilities will have relatively more potential for adding intrinsic value to put option positions than stocks with relatively low volatilities. In general, put options on high-volatility stocks should have relatively higher prices than those written on lower-volatility stocks.

RELATIONSHIP TO TIME TO MATURITY Since put options, like call options, are depleting assets, their behavior over time is similar to that of call options. Put options written on the same stock with equivalent exercise prices will differ in price according to maturity. Longer-term put options will have higher prices. Further, at-the-money put options will have the largest time premiums and far-from-the-money put options the smallest. The put option's time premium will slowly decay until about 45 days until maturity; after that, the decay process will accelerate. Exhibit 2-4 graphically depicts the decay process for at-the-money and out-of-the-money put options.

Properties of Option Prices

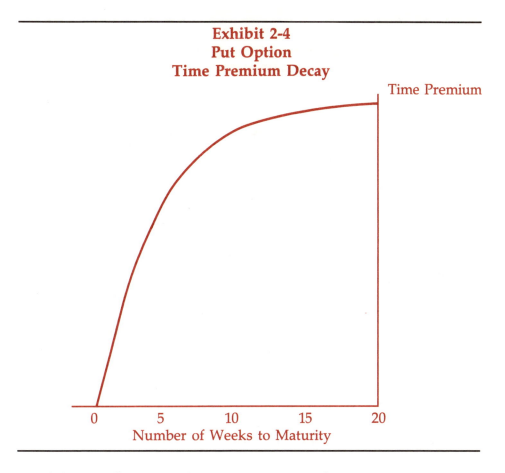

**Exhibit 2-4
Put Option
Time Premium Decay**

Exhibit 2-5 illustrates the time premiums for IBM put options. It is easiest to see how the time premium increases with maturity by examining the out-of-the-money put options. Note how the IBM 130 and IBM 135 put options increase in value with maturity. The November and January IBM 145 put options demonstrate how the time premium shrinks as put options go far-from-the-money. Both of these have 9½ points of intrinsic value (145 − 135½) and relatively small time premiums: ¼ point for the November options (9¾ − 9½) and 1 point for the January options (10½ − 9½).

The October IBM 145 put option appears to be underpriced and is an example of a situation that all investors encounter at one time or another. Theoretically, the October IBM 145 put option should be selling for at least its intrinsic value of 9½, not its quoted value

---

Exhibit 2-5
Put Option Price Quotations
WSJ, 9/26/86

Option and N.Y. Close		Striking Price	Puts—Last		
			Oct.	Nov.	Jan.
IBM	135½	130	$^{13}/_{16}$	2	3¼
	135½	135	$2^7/_{16}$	4¼	5⅛
	135½	140	5⅝	6½	8
	135½	145	9	9¾	10½

---

of 9. Since it is quoted at ½ point under parity, it appears that a sure profit of ½ point per share of IBM can be earned by purchasing the October IBM 145 for 9, purchasing IBM shares for 135½, and then exercising the put option by selling the shares at 145 [½ = 145 − (9 + 135½)]. Unfortunately, this will probably be impossible, since it is not known whether IBM stock actually was trading at 135½ when the October 145 put option traded at 9. It may be that the last October IBM 145 was traded long before IBM stock reached a price of 135½. On the other hand, even if shares of IBM stock and the October 145 put option did trade simultaneously, professional traders and arbitrageurs would have capitalized on the mispricing situation and theoretically consistent option prices would have been restored in a matter of minutes because of the trading strategy outlined above. Thus, when grossly mispriced options appear in the newspaper, rest assured that any available profits have already been captured by professional investors and speculators.

RELATIONSHIP TO EXERCISE PRICE   The relationship between the fifth pricing factor—the exercise price—and the put option's price is positive and occurs because put options gain intrinsic value as exercise prices increase. Thus, put options written on a given stock with identical maturity dates will increase in value with their exercise prices. Conversely, put options with low exercise prices have low intrinsic values. This can be clearly seen in Exhibit 2-5 by reading down any of the maturity columns.

Properties of Option Prices

RELATIONSHIP TO INTEREST RATES   An inverse relationship exists between put option prices and the sixth pricing factor, unanticipated changes in interest rates. This relationship can be explained by focusing on put option buyers. A put option holder owns the right to the cash flow generated by the exercise price. An unanticipated increase in interest rates imposes an opportunity cost on the put option buyer, since he or she lacks the cash on hand with which to take advantage of the higher rates. Therefore, put options become less desirable, and their premiums are bid down in the marketplace.

It is also possible to explain this inverse relationship using a present-value argument. Specifically, the put option premium reflects the present value of the exercise price, where the present value is computed by discounting the put option's exercise price from maturity to the current time period. Lower interest rates increase the present value of the put option's exercise price and thus increase intrinsic value. Higher intrinsic values translate into higher put option prices. If interest rates increase, the discounted present value of the exercise price drops, resulting in lower intrinsic values and lower put option prices.

Earlier it was emphasized that the relationship between interest rates and call options is predictable if stock prices remain unchanged. The same holds true for put options. One should not expect higher put option prices when interest rates decrease if the price of the underlying stock rises. The stock price must remain fixed in order for this relationship to be predictable.

OPTION DELTAS

This section focuses on a useful tool that is based on the relationships between the six key pricing factors and option prices: the delta.

DEFINITION OF DELTA   An option's *delta* may be defined as a measure of how an option's price will change if the underlying stock's price experiences a small change and the other pricing factors are assumed to remain stable. The delta is simply the practical application of the relationship between the price of the underlying stock and the option's price. Since call options have a positive relationship and put options a negative relationship with the underlying stock's price, call option deltas will be positive and put option deltas negative. Indeed, since the put option is the obverse of the call option, its delta can be computed by subtracting 1 from the call option's delta.

Call option deltas range in value from 0 to 1, while put option deltas take values of from 0 to −1. At-the-money call and put options have deltas of approximately +½ and −½, respectively. As options go deep-in-the-money and gain intrinsic value, the delta's absolute value approaches 1. Thus, deep-in-the-money call options have deltas that approximate +1 and deep-in-the-money put options deltas of approximately −1. Both deep-out-of-the-money put options and call options have deltas that are virtually zero.

The various delta values reflect the strength of the relationship between the option and the underlying stock. A deep-in-the-money call option with a delta of 1 has a strong positive relationship with the underlying stock and will experience a $1 price increase for each $1 gain in the stock's price. Conversely, the value of a deep-in-the-money put option that has a delta of −1 and, hence, a strong inverse relationship with the underlying stock will increase in value by $1 for every $1 loss experienced by the stock. This price behavior is not surprising, since the premiums for deep-in-the-money options are composed almost entirely of intrinsic value. Moreover, these options are virtually perfect surrogates for positions in the underlying stock, with long call options mimicking long stock positions and long put options imitating short stock positions. Options that are deep-out-of-the-money have no intrinsic value, a weak relationship with the underlying stock, extremely small deltas, and little chance of being transformed into stock positions by the option owner. At-the-money options have no intrinsic value but do have the potential to become profitable surrogate stock positions for the option owner. Therefore, the delta values of ½, in absolute value, will reflect this profit potential.

DELTA-NEUTRAL POSITIONS   An option's delta is also important for its risk management capability. The delta provides the investor with the number of shares needed, in combination with the option, to construct a position that will be insulated from the effects

Properties of Option Prices   37

of small price movements in the underlying stock. When an investor combines options and stock to create such a position, the position is said to be *delta neutral*. The total value of the position will remain stable even though the values of the individual components will change. The following example illustrates these concepts.

Assume that Kellogg's common stock is trading at 51½ and the 4-month put options and call options, with striking prices of 50, have values of 2 and 4¾, respectively. Assume too that the call option's delta is .63 and the put option's delta is −.37 (.63 − 1.00). These data imply that a $1 increase in the price of a stock will result in a $.63 increase in the call option's price and a $.37 decrease in the put option's price. Further, a delta-neutral call position can be created by purchasing 63 shares of Kellogg stock for every call option sold, while a delta-neutral put position can be obtained by purchasing 37 shares of stock for every put option purchased. Since stock price changes cause call option prices to change in the same direction, one must take opposite positions in the call option and shares of stock to insulate the combined position from the underlying stock's price changes. The opposite directional change in the put option price that results from the stock price change dictates that similar positions be taken in the put option and the shares of stock to shield the combined position from the effects of the stock price changes.

Exhibits 2-6 and 2-7 illustrate the behavior of these delta-neutral positions. Exhibit 2-6 shows how the value of a total position, composed of a Kellogg call option and shares of Kellogg common stock, remains stable as stock and option prices change. Exhibit 2-7 presents the behavior of the Kellogg put option and stock position. Note that the values of the total positions remain stable because of each component's proportions. The key to understanding delta-neutral positions lies in realizing that the effects of the stock price changes are neutralized by the relative proportions of the position's components.

PROFIT GRAPHS FOR BASIC INVESTMENT POSITIONS

The final section of this chapter presents and explains profit graphs for the six basic investment positions:

38   Chapter 2

1. Long the stock
2. Short the stock
3. Long the call option
4. Short the call option
5. Long the put option
6. Short the put option

These graphs and the accompanying discussions will serve two purposes. First, they should solidify one's understanding of the profit

---

Exhibit 2-6
Delta Neutral Call Option Positions

Kellogg Common Stock	Kellogg 50 Calls	Component Values	Position Values
51½	Delta .63 Price 4.75	Short 1 call @ 475 Long 63 shares @ 51½	−475 +3,244.50
			Net long 2,769.50
52½	Delta .63 Price 4.75 + .63 = 5.38	Short 1 call @ 538 Long 63 shares @ 52½	−538 +3,307.50
			Net long 2,769.50
50½	Delta .63 Price 4.75 − .63 = 4.12	Short 1 call @ 412 Long 63 shares @ 50½	−412 +3,181.50
			Net long 2,769.50

Exhibit 2-7
Delta Neutral Put Option Positions

Kellogg Common Stock	Kellogg 50 Puts	Component Values	Position Values
51½	Delta .37 Price 2.00	Long 1 put @ 200 Long 37 shares @ 51½	+200 +1,905.50
			Net long 2,105.50
52½	Delta .37 Price 2.00 − .37 = 1.63	Long 1 put @ 163 Long 37 shares @ 52½	+163 +1,942.50
			Net long 2,105.50
50½	Delta .37 Price 2.00 + .37 = 2.37	Long 1 put @ 237 Long 37 shares @ 50½	+237 +1,868.50
			Net long 2,105.50

Properties of Option Prices 39

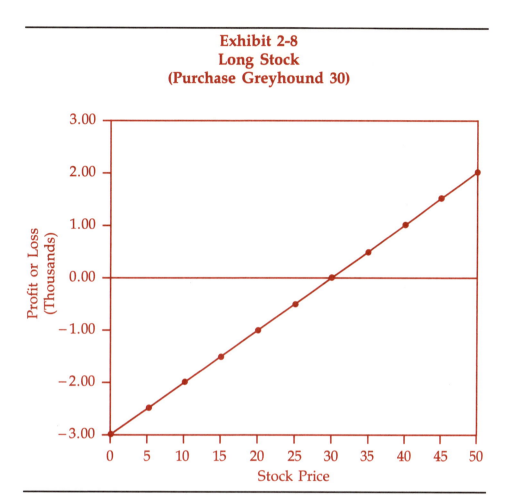

**Exhibit 2-8
Long Stock
(Purchase Greyhound 30)**

and loss potential of the various positions. Second, they will provide a foundation for understanding the more complex strategies that will be discussed in later chapters.

LONG STOCK POSITION Exhibit 2-8 depicts a long position in 100 shares of Greyhound common stock where the purchase price is $30 per share, or $3,000 for the total position. As the share price of Greyhound stock rises, the position's profit accrues at a rate of $100 per $1 increase in the stock's price. Note that if the price of Greyhound stock drops to zero, the maximum loss of $3,000 is incurred. There is no maximum profit, since there is no upper limit on the stock's price.

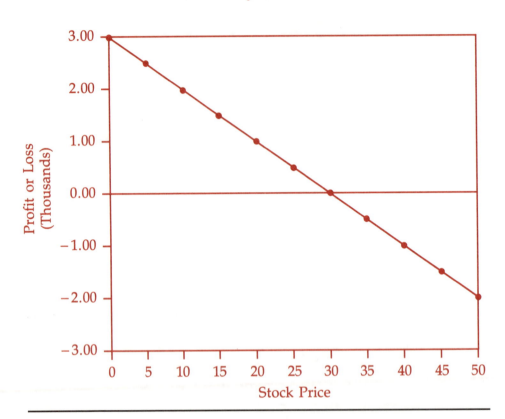

SHORT STOCK POSITION A short position in 100 shares of Greyhound common stock is portrayed in Exhibit 2-9. Here the investor is attempting to capitalize on an anticipated per-share price decline from its current level of $30. The rate of change in this short position's value is identical to that in the long position's value: $100 per $1 change in the price of Greyhound common stock. The maximum profit the short seller can earn is $3,000 if Greyhound stock becomes worthless. There is no maximum loss, since there is no upper limit on the price of Greyhound shares. Thus, it is theoretically possible for the short seller to suffer an infinite loss—an extremely risky position.

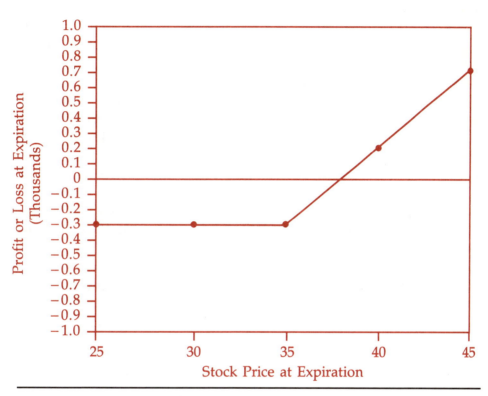

LONG CALL OPTION POSITION Exhibit 2-10 illustrates the profit and loss potential of buying a Greyhound call option and then holding it to maturity. In this example, the call option has an exercise price of $35 and a premium of 3 points, or $300. If the call option expires at-the-money or out-of-the-money, the maximum loss of $300 will be incurred. The call option must be 3 points in-the-money, with a share price equal to $38, for the investor to break even. For share prices greater than $38, the long call option is profitable because by exercising the call option, shares can be purchased for $35 and then sold at the higher market price. There is no upper limit on the call option's profit, since there is no upper limit on the price of Greyhound stock. Remember that if one hopes to earn unlimited profits and invests one's total wealth in a long call option position, one also runs the risk of total ruin within a short time span.

SHORT CALL OPTION POSITION Exhibit 2-11 illustrates the profit potential of writing *uncovered* or *naked* call options on K-Mart stock. A short position is taken in a K-Mart call option that controls 100 shares of K-Mart stock, has a striking price of 50, and a premium of 5 points, or $500. If the naked call option is at-the-money or out-of-the-money at maturity, it will expire worthless and the option writer will keep the entire $500 premium as profit. However, if the price of K-Mart stock rises, the option will experience large losses as the stock price moves past the breakeven point of $55. At this point, the in-the-money call option becomes worthwhile for its owner to exercise against the writer. Since the writer does not own shares of K-Mart stock, he or she must purchase them in the market at the prevailing price. The greater the current market price, the more the writer must pay to acquire K-Mart shares that will be delivered to the call option buyer at the striking price of $55 per share. Since there is no upper limit on the stock price, there is no upper limit on the naked call option writer's potential loss. However, note that the naked call writer's profit is limited to the amount of the premium taken in when the call option was sold—again a very risky position.

LONG PUT OPTION POSITION The profit potential of a long position in a K-Mart put option is illustrated in Exhibit 2-12. The put option controls 100 shares of K-Mart stock, has a striking price of $50, and can be purchased for 5 points, or $500. If the price of K-Mart stock falls to zero, the put option owner will exercise the option and force the put option writer to pay $5,000 for 100 shares of worthless K-Mart stock. The put option owner will earn a profit of $4,500 from this transaction—the $5,000 exercise price minus the $500 put option premium. If the price of K-Mart stock is greater than or equal to the put option's exercise price of $50 at maturity, the put option will expire worthless and the owner will forfeit the $500 premium. This position is less cumbersome and less risky than a short position in K-Mart stock. However, even if one is positive that a large price decline in K-Mart stock is imminent, one should be

Properties of Option Prices

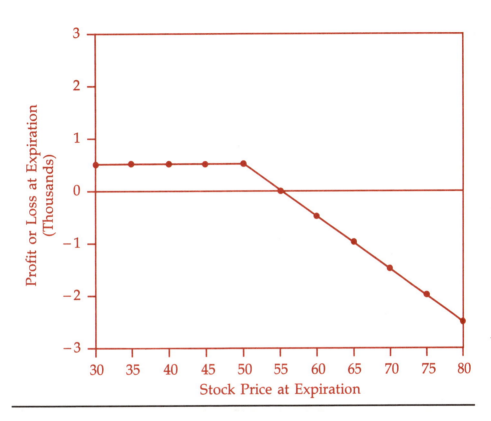

Exhibit 2-11
Short Call
(K-Mart 50 Call)

prudent and refrain from investing one's total wealth in these put options, since the possibility of total ruin looms large.

SHORT PUT OPTION POSITION Our final profit graph is Exhibit 2-13, which portrays the profit potential for a K-Mart put option writer. The parameters are identical to those of the long K-Mart put option position: The put option controls 100 shares of K-Mart stock, the striking price is $50, and the premium is $500. The put option writer collects the $500 premium and hopes that the stock price will be greater than or equal to the striking price of $50 at the option's expiration. Under these conditions, the put option

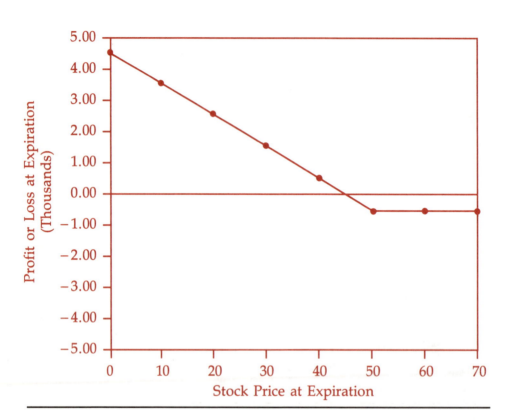

Exhibit 2-12
Long Put
(K-Mart 50 Put)

will have no value for its owner and the writer will profit by the $500 premium. However, if the stock price is less than $45 at expiration, the put option owner will profit and the put option writer will lose. The maximum loss the put option writer can suffer is $4,500, the value of the exercise price less the amount of the original premium. Note that the writer runs the risk of losing $4,500 for a maximum profit of $500, the amount paid to the writer when the put option was sold. Theoretically, the maximum loss for the put option writer is less than the naked call option writer's loss. Practically speaking, however, the potential consequences of an adverse

Properties of Option Prices

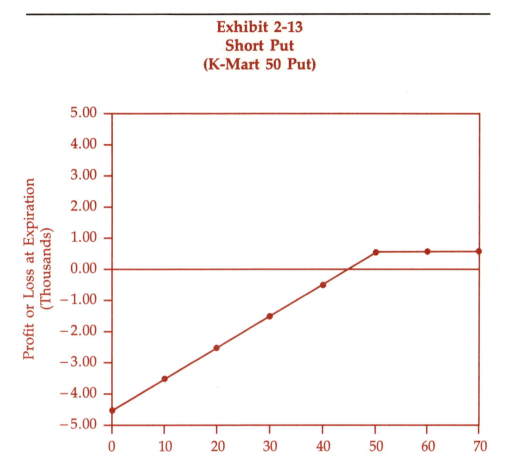

**Exhibit 2-13
Short Put
(K-Mart 50 Put)**

movement in the stock price for both unsecured option writers are extremely severe: total ruin.

CONCLUSION

This chapter explored the relationships of call option prices and put option prices to the six basic option pricing factors: the underlying stock's price, the stock's dividends, the stock's price volatility, the time until the option expires, the option's exercise price, and interest rates. The discussion of these relationships was based on the concepts of intrinsic value, parity, and time premium. The chapter ended with a graphical presentation of the six basic investment positions: long the stock, short the stock, long the call option, short the call option, long the put option, and short the put option. The purpose of these graphs was to reinforce the concepts of risk and return and to prepare the reader for the more complex strategies that will be introduced in subsequent chapters.

Chapter Three

SIMPLE CALL OPTION STRATEGIES

PURCHASING CALL OPTIONS VERSUS PURCHASING STOCK

Recall that call options give the purchaser the right to buy stock at a predetermined price (the striking price) between the date of purchase and the option's expiration date. A call option is usually purchased with the hope that the underlying security will increase in value. Usually the call option's price will increase as the underlying security's price goes up. The purchase of call options is considered a bullish strategy and is used to obtain greater leverage while limiting the investor's risk of loss. Purchasing call options alone is purely speculative, since options are a depleting asset—that is, their value diminishes over time if the underlying stock does nothing.

When an investor owns stock in a company—even a very small percentage—he or she in effect owns equity in that corporation. If the value of the stock decreases, the investor is under no time constraints to recoup losses. With a call option, on the other hand, the investor must hope that the underlying stock will move in his or her favor and increase in value by the time the call option expires.

Exhibit 3-1 compares the purchase of an at-the-money call option with a striking price of 45 and the purchase of a stock at $45 a share. (In the Exhibits to follow, the thin line represents stock purchase on short sale, and the thick line represents option strategy.) As you can

49

see, the loss on the call is limited to the call's purchase price of $250, which is significantly less than the potential loss on the stock at $4,500. In addition, the call provides greater leverage since the call buyer has committed much less money than the stock purchaser. In order to fully understand this concept, let us consider a real-world situation.

Suppose that the economy in general seems to be rebounding and it appears that manufacturing companies will also show some type of recovery. You want to speculate on improved earnings for Chrysler Corporation. You know that Chrysler common stock is trading at $35 a share and the call options are priced as follows:

Chrysler 6-month 30 call, 8½ points
Chrysler 6-month 35 call, 3½ points
Chrysler 6-month 40 call, 1½ points

For example, a 6-month at-the-money call is selling at 3½ points, or $350 for the right to buy 100 shares of Chrysler stock at 35.

Now suppose your economic scenario proves to be correct and Chrysler stock goes up 5 points in just a few months to 40 for a 14.3 percent gain [5 points (profit)/35 (stock purchase price)]. At the same time, the call price increases from 3½ to 7½ (5 points intrinsic value and 2½ points time value) for a gain of 114 percent in the same time period [4-point increase in option/3½ (purchase price)]. As an investor in this call option, you could either sell it in the options market to realize your gain or exercise your right to buy 100 shares of Chrysler stock at $35 per share. Your decision will be based on whether you want to actually own the underlying stock or just take part in the quick move.

If your economic scenario was incorrect and you bought 100 shares of Chrysler stock, your downside risk theoretically would be 35 points. It is very unlikely that the shares of Chrysler stock would fall to zero. However, the point is that if you were speculating on a quick upturn rather than investing for the long term, the purchase of the 6-month at-the-money call might meet your speculative objectives more directly and limit your downside risk by the amount of the option—in this case, $350 as opposed to $3,500. It would also offer you potentially *greater leverage*.

If you wanted to be very speculative, you could buy 10 six-month at-the-money call options for 3½ points, or $3,500. Then, if Chrysler

Simple Call Option Strategies

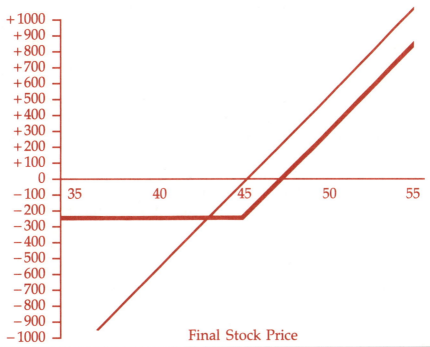

Exhibit 3-1
Buy At-the-Money Call with a Striking Price of 45 at 2½ or $250

moves up 5 points to 40, you will make $4,000 (4-point increase in option × number of options, or 10) as compared to $500 had you only bought 100 shares of Chrysler stock in anticipation of a quick move in the stock price. However, if Chrysler stock remains flat or goes down, you will lose your entire $3,500 investment.

TIME CONSIDERATIONS

In the above investment situation, we compared purchasing a stock at 35 with buying a 6-month at-the-money call option. However, this situation rarely occurs in everyday life. Usually an investor must decide between the purchase of an out-of-the-money or in-the-money call option. Our next consideration is how much time value to buy—three, six, or nine months.

Typically, a speculator purchases the cheapest call option available, which, of course, would be the nearest-term out-of-the-money option. This might be the appropriate strategy if one were expecting a major move in the stock within a relatively short period. However, the dollar price alone should not be the determining factor in deciding whether or not to purchase a particular call option. Some people look at it from a purely economic perspective, namely that they may lose only a small amount of money but enjoy a potential for large gains. The point to keep in mind is that even though an out-of-the-money call option provides the greatest amount of leverage, the purchaser has a greater chance of losing all of his or her money. Also, if the stock rises only moderately, an in-the-money call option may outperform an out-of-the-money option.

Returning to the Chrysler example, it is clear that if you purchased the out-of-the-money 40 call option at 1½, you would lose your entire investment unless Chrysler stock rose above 40 during the option's life. However, if you bought the in-the-money 30 call option at 6½, you would need only a rise in the stock price to above 36½ in order to make a profit. In this example, you would have more dollars at risk by purchasing the in-the-money call option than by buying the out-of-the-money call option, which is why you must assess the amount of dollar exposure you are willing to assume in any option purchase decision.

Let us return to the decision of whether to purchase a 3-, 6-, or 9-month call option. As mentioned earlier, investors often purchase the nearest-term call option simply because it is the cheapest. However, the decision should initially be based on how quickly the investor thinks the underlying stock will increase in value.

If the investor is not confident that the increase will take place in the very near term, he or she should attempt to purchase the next-furthest-out call option in order to minimize the risk. If the investor thinks that the underlying stock is going to move up immediately, the nearest-term call option may be the best choice. When making this decision, it is important to remember that if a stock stays stagnant, the call options will maintain their time value on a consistent basis up until the last six weeks prior to expiration. This is when the most rapid deterioration in the option's time value will occur.

Simple Call Option Strategies

PURCHASING A CALL OPTION
WITH AN EXISTING PROFIT IN THE STOCK

Another situation in which the purchase of call options may meet the investor's objectives and limit risk occurs when the investor is faced with taking a profit on a stock. For example, suppose you purchased Abbott Labs stock at $45 a share and doubled your money one year later. You still like Abbott Labs, but you think the stock may pull back and you wouldn't mind taking a profit. At the same time, you feel that the stock has some more upside potential because some of Abbott's new products are awaiting FDA approval that, when obtained, could add substantially to its earnings. In this situation, you could sell your stock and use a small percentage of your profits to purchase a call option in the event there is additional upside potential. You would then be able to partake in any additional gains yet have much less money at risk if there is a substantial fall in the stock's price.

OPTION DELTAS

In Chapter Two, we discussed how an option's delta measures how much the option will move relative to the near-term movement of the underlying stock. The deeper in-the-money a call option is, the closer to 1 the delta will be. Note too that as the option's time value erodes, so does its delta if the underlying stock price remains unchanged. However, for deep in-the-money options, the delta may increase as maturity approaches. The delta on a particular stock option can be obtained from a variety of services, including brokers.

Deltas clearly are an excellent tool to use when deciding which call option to purchase. For example, suppose that XYZ Corporation stock is trading at 25. The 3-month 25 call option might have a delta of .50 and the 3-month 30 call option a delta of .25. If the stock rises by 1 point, the 25 call option will probably move up one-half of a point and the 30 call option one-quarter of a point. If you want to purchase a call option that will mimic the stock price movement, you should buy the one with the highest delta.

NAKED CALL WRITING

Writing or selling call options without owning the underlying stock is a bearish strategy known as *naked call writing.* Here the seller or writer of a call option receives the option premium from the buyer and incurs an obligation to sell the stock at the striking price. If the stock is below the striking price at expiration, the call option will expire worthless and the writer will have earned the premium as profit. If the stock is above the striking price, the buyer may exercise the call option and force the writer to sell the stock to him or her at the striking price. The writer's loss will be the stock's market price less the striking price less the premium received. The uncovered writer may, however, cancel the obligation at any time prior to the assignment by purchasing a call option with the same striking price and expiration date in the market through a broker, thus closing out the short position.

For example, suppose that XYZ Corporation common stock is trading at $45 a share and the call options are priced as follows:

XYZ 3-month 40 call, 5¾ points
XYZ 3-month 45 call, 2½ points
XYZ 6-month 50 call, ¾ points

If you think the price of XYZ Corporation stock is going to fall and sell the 3-month at-the-money call option for the 2½-point premium, you will incur an obligation to sell 100 shares of XYZ at 45 a share within the next 3 months. If the stock is below 45 at expiration, the option will expire worthless. Thus, you will have earned 2½ points, or $250. However, your risk is unlimited, since you will still be obligated to sell the stock to the call option purchaser at $45 per share upon demand. This is shown in Exhibit 3-2. If the stock price ran up to 80 on takeover speculation and you did not own the underlying stock, you would have to go into the marketplace and purchase it at the current market price. In this case, you would buy XYZ Corporation stock at 80, or $8,000 for 100 shares, and sell it to the person who exercised the call option at 45, or $4,500 for 100 shares. In this example, you would have a loss of $3,250: $8,000 (market price) – $4,500 (striking price) – $250 (option premium). The seller could take a little less risk for less premium by selling a further-out call

Simple Call Option Strategies 55

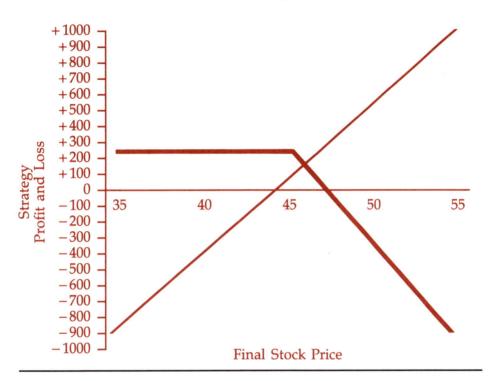

Exhibit 3-2
Sell At-the-Money Call with a Striking Price of 45 at 2½ or $250

option. In this scenario, you could have sold the 3-month 50 call option for a premium of ¾, which would obligate you to sell XYZ Corporation stock to the call option purchaser for $50.

These are not necessarily attractive strategies for the average investor, since one takes a very large risk for a relatively small reward (the premium). They are, however, important to understand when looking at our next strategy: covered call option writing.

COVERED CALL OPTION WRITING

In previous discussions, we noted that options are a depleting asset. If the underlying stock is stagnant over time, the out-of-the-money

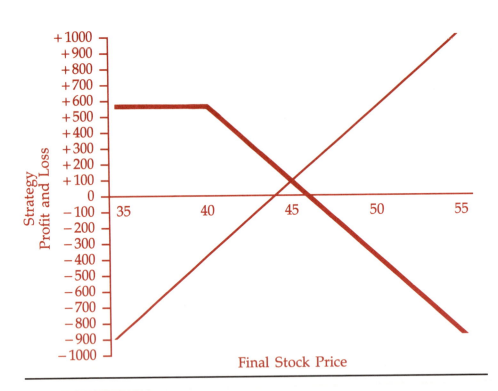

**Exhibit 3-3
Sell In-the-Money Call with a Striking Price of 40 at 5¾ or $575**

call option will expire worthless. When writing a covered call option, the investor buys a stock that he or she is comfortable owning and sells or writes a call option against that position.

We strongly recommend that you pick this stock based on its fundamental merits and not just because the returns promised by the strategy look attractive. The covered call option writing strategy reduces your downside risk by the amount of the premium that you received from the option's sale. At the same time, you will have limited your upside potential gain by the striking price at which you have agreed to sell the stock. This is a bullish strategy, which in fact is more conservative than the outright purchase of the stock because you will reduce your downside risk by the amount of the

Simple Call Option Strategies

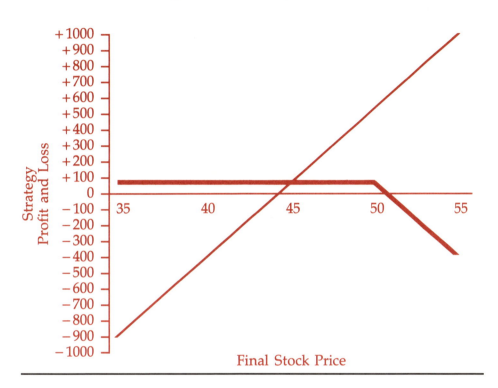

Exhibit 3-4
Sell Out-the-Money Call with a Striking Price of 50 at ¾ or $75

premium. At the same time, you will realize additional income if the stock does nothing.

The covered call option writing strategy will outperform the outright stock purchase in three situations: If the stock (1) falls, (2) remains the same, or (3) rises slightly. The only time the outright purchase of the stock will outperform the covered call option writing strategy is when the stock price increases dramatically during the call option's life. When determining which call option to write, you should understand that writing in-the-money call options may offer more downside protection but may also fail to offer you the upside potential you are seeking. Conversely, an out-of-the-money

Exhibit 3-5
Buy Stock at 45 or $4,500; Sell In-the-Money Call with a Striking Price of 40 at 5¾ or $575

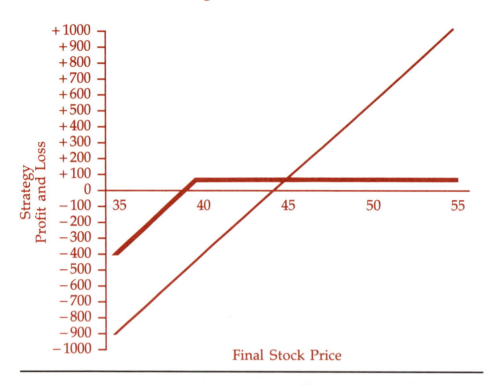

covered write may offer you a higher potential yield but less downside protection than an in-the-money covered call write.

The following sections will help explain this point by presenting graphic depictions of three covered write situations on the same stock.

IN-THE-MONEY COVERED CALL WRITE In Exhibit 3-5, the investor has purchased 100 shares of a stock for $45 a share and sold an in-the-money call option with a striking price of 40 for 5¾ (5 points intrinsic value, ¾ point time value), or $575. From the graph, it is evident that the investor has 5¾ points of downside protection (striking price − current stock price + call option premium) but an upside potential of only ¾ point, which is the time value of the call option.

Simple Call Option Strategies

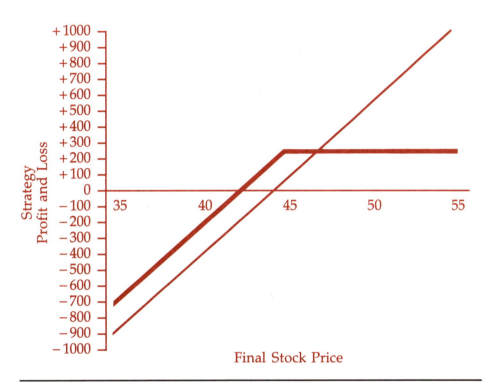

**Exhibit 3-6
Buy Stock at 45 or $4,500; Sell At-the-Money Call
with a Striking Price of 45 at 2½ or $250**

AT-THE-MONEY COVERED CALL WRITE In Exhibit 3-6, the investor has purchased 100 shares of the same stock for $45 a share and sold an at-the-money call option with a striking price of 45 for 2½ (all time value), or $250. The graph makes it clear that the investor has 2½ points of downside protection (striking price − current stock price + call option premium) and 2½ points of upside potential, which is the premium from the at-the-money call. This offers less downside protection but more upside potential than the in-the-money covered call option situation.

Exhibit 3-7
Buy Stock at 45 or $4,500; Sell Out-of-the-Money Call with a Striking Price of 50 at ¾ or $75

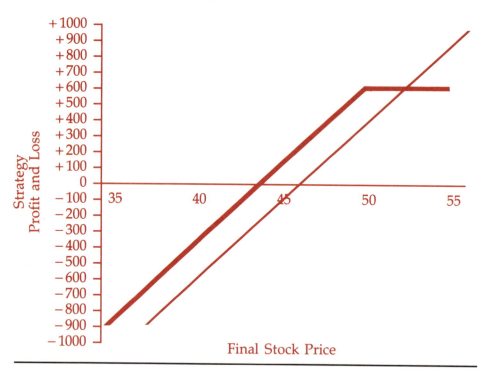

OUT-OF-THE-MONEY COVERED CALL WRITE In Exhibit 3-7, the investor has purchased 100 shares of the same stock for $45 a share and sold an out-of-the-money call option with a striking price of 50 for ¾ point (all time premium), or $75. From the graph, it is evident that the investor has ¾ point of downside protection and upside potential of 5¾ points (striking price − current stock price + call option premium). Clearly this offers more upside potential but less downside protection than the other two covered call option situations.

AN ILLUSTRATION Now that we have essentially defined covered call option writing, let's take a look at some realistic situations and their possible consequences.

Simple Call Option Strategies

American Brands (AMB) looks like a very attractive investment. Its stock is currently selling for $45 a share and pays a $2.08 annual dividend for a yield of 4.6 percent ($2.08 dividend/$45 stock price). The call options are priced as follows:

AMB 6-month 45 call, 4 points
AMB 6-month 50 call, 2 points
AMB 6-month 40 call, 7 points

If you thought the stock was going to move upward in a fairly short time, you would just purchase the stock or a call option. However, since you are not a good market or stock timer, an alternative to an outright purchase of American Brands stock would be to buy the stock and sell a 6-month 50 call option for a premium of 2 points. This would give you 2 points of additional income or some downside protection, which would give you an effective cost basis of 43: $45 (market price) – $2 (call option premium). If the stock ran up and exceeded the striking price of 50 at expiration, it would be called away and your return would be 7 points (striking price – cost basis), or a 15 percent capital gain (7-point gain/$45 original cost). On an annualized basis, it would be a return of 30 percent (15[pc] × (12 months/6 months) plus any dividends you might have received in that six-month period.

In order to give you an even more accurate picture, we have provided an illustrative covered call writing worksheet for our example. This will allow you to accurately compute the cost basis, the return if the stock is called away, the return if the stock remains unchanged, and the breakeven or downside protection. Exhibit 3-8 is a standard worksheet format. Exhibit 3-9 shows the same worksheet with data supplied for our American Brands example.

In our original example, we did not compute the returns including the dividends on AMB. The worksheet in Exhibit 3-9 shows that if you include the dividends, your return increases by more than 7 percent, or 37.5 percent annualized. In this scenario, the largest risk you have taken for the locked-in return is the possibility that the stock will have a tremendous run-up and you will not take part in the profit above the $50 striking price.

It should be noted that although you made an obligation to sell American Brands stock at 50, you may cancel that obligation by purchasing an identical call option in the market through a broker for a closing transaction. Let us look at a couple of scenarios in which you might want to consider this alternative.

Exhibit 3-8
Sample Covered Call Writing Worksheet

1. Stock:
2. Dividends (quarterly):
3. Days until expiration:

A. Initial Position

Buy _____ shares of _____ @ _____ .
    #   stock   price

  Add commissions
  Total cost of stock   (A) _____

Sell _____ calls _____ / _____ @ _____ .
   #   exp.   striking
      month   price

  Deduct commissions
Net proceeds from sale of calls   (B) _____

Net investment [(A) – (B)]   (C) _____

B. Return If Stock Is Above the Striking Price at Expiration

Sell _____ shares of _____ @ _____ .
   #   stock   striking
          price

  Deduct commissions
Net proceeds from sale of stock   _____
Add dividends received

_____ × _____ × _____   (D) _____
Dividend # of div. # of shares

Total balance   (E) _____

Net profit [(E) – (C)]   (F) _____

Percentage return [(F) / (C)]   (G) _____

Annualized return [365 / #3 × (G)]   _____

Simple Call Option Strategies

C. Return If Stock Is Unchanged at Expiration

Net option income (B) _____
+
Dividends received (D) _____

Total income (H) _____

Total Cost of Stock (A) _____

Rate of return [(H) / (A)] (I) _____

Annualized rate of return _____
  [365 / #3 × (I)]

D. Downside Protection or Breakeven Point on Stock

Total cost of stock (A) _____

Less proceeds from sale of calls (B) _____

Less dividends received (D) _____

Subtotal (I) _____
  − Adjusted cost for stock
Divide by number of shares / _____

Breakeven price per share = _____

Exhibit 3-9
Covered Call Writing Worksheet for American Brands

1. Stock: **American Brands**
2. Dividends (quarterly): **.52**
3. Days until expiration: **182**

A. Initial Position

Buy **300** shares of **AMB** @ **45** .
    #   stock   price

    Add commissions
    Total cost of stock (A) **13,500**

Sell **3** calls **March** / **50** @ **2** .
   #   exp.   striking   month   price

64   Chapter 3

    Deduct commissions
Net proceeds from sale of calls   (B) __**600**__

Net investment [(A) − (B)]   (C) __**12,900**__

B.   Return If Stock Is Above the Striking Price at Expiration

Sell __**300**__ shares of __**AMB**__ @ __**50**__ .
     #   stock   striking
                                    price

    Deduct commissions
Net proceeds from sale of stock   __**15,000**__
Add dividends received

$$\frac{.52}{\text{Dividend}} \times \frac{2}{\text{\# of div.}} \times \frac{300}{\text{\# of shares}}$$ (D) __**312**__

Total balance   (E) __**15,312**__

Net profit [(E) − (C)]   (F) __**2,412**__

Percentage return [(F) / (C)]   (G) __**18.7%**__

Annualized return [365 / #3 × (G)]   __**37.5%**__

C.   Return If Stock Is Unchanged at Expiration
Net option income   (B) __**600**__
                                            +
Dividends received   (D) __**312**__

Total income   (H) __**912**__

Total Cost of Stock   (A) __**13,500**__

Rate of return [(H) / (A)]   (I) __**6.8%**__

Annualized rate of return   __**13.6%**__
  [365 / #3 × (I)]

D.   Downside Protection or Breakeven Point on Stock
Total cost of stock   (A) __**13,500**__

Less proceeds from sale of calls   (B) __**600**__

Less dividends received   (D) __**312**__

Simple Call Option Strategies   65

Subtotal	(I)	**12,588**
– Adjusted cost for stock		
Divide by number of shares	/	**300**
Breakeven price per share	=	**41.96**

ROLLING UP   Suppose the stock ran up to 52 for a 15.5 percent increase over five months [(52 – 45) / 45)] and the options were now priced as follows:

AMB March 45 call, 7½ points
AMB March 50 call, 3 points
AMB March 55 call, 1½ points

The 50 call option that you originally sold for 2 is now worth 3 with one month until expiration. Two points of the premium are intrinsic value, and the remaining point is the option's time value. Further, the 4-month June call options are priced as follows:

AMB June 45 call, 8½ points
AMB June 50 call, 4 points
AMB June 55 call, 2 points

The AMB June 55 call is selling for 2 points, which is composed entirely of time value.

At this point, you may elect to close the original position by purchasing an AMB 50 call option for 3, which would result in a 1-point loss. However, you may now sell a 4-month 55 call option for 2 points. Now you will have increased your cost basis by one more point to 46 [45 (original cost) – 2 (original option sold) + 3 (repurchase of original option) – 1 (sell 55 call)] from 45 and made an obligation to sell the stock at 55. If the stock is called away when the option expires in four months, your capital gain will be 15.2 percent [(55 – 46)/46], or 30.4 percent annualized. By closing the position in the AMB 50 and selling the XYZ 55, you will have rolled up to the call option with the next higher striking price. Note that we have not included dividends.

This follow-up strategy is known as *rolling up* and is defined as buying back the call option that you originally sold and simultaneously selling a call option with a higher striking price.

You may also sell an option that expires at a later date than the original, allowing you to take in additional time premium. If you thought that American Brands was a takeover candidate, you may have decided not to sell the 55 call option and just hold the stock. Nevertheless, it is important to understand the rolling-up concept.

ROLLING DOWN There are also times when you may choose to roll down. *Rolling down* is defined as buying back the call option that you originally sold and simultaneously selling a call option with a lower striking price. Again you may opt to sell an option with a further-out expiration date than the original option's in order to take in additional time premium.

To illustrate, suppose that AMB dropped from 45 to 40 over 5 months. Now the 50 call that originally was sold for 2 is trading at ¼ point, and the 4-month June call options are priced as follows:

AMB June 40 call, 2 points
AMB June 45 call, 1½ points
AMB June 50 call, ¾ points

You could roll down by purchasing the AMB 50 for ¼ and sell a 4-month AMB June 45 call for 1½. Then the cost basis on the stock would be 41¾ [45 (original cost) − 2 (original option sold) + ¼ (repurchase of original option) − 1½ (sell 45 call)], with an obligation to sell it at 45. This would be an appropriate move if you thought the stock was going to stay flat or rise slightly. If you felt the stock was going to continue dropping, you should have just sold the stock. In this situation, your loss is less than it would be had you just purchased the stock because you sold the original call for 2 points, which gave you some downside protection.

SELLING CALL OPTIONS AGAINST A STOCK WITH AN EXISTING PROFIT

There is yet another way to use calls in conjunction with stock as a tool for increasing your yield. For example, suppose you like ABC Corporation stock, which is currently at $30 a share. You have little interest in selling calls against it, because you think the next few

Simple Call Option Strategies 67

quarters are going to be exceptionally strong from an earnings stand-point. Six months later, the stock indeed has reacted to favorable earnings: It has increased 40 percent in value to $42 a share, and the 3-month 45 call is trading at $3 a share.

At this point the market looks skittish, and you are not sure whether ABC stock can continue its upward momentum. You could either put in a stop-loss order or just sell the stock, but another alter-native would be to sell the 45 call option for 3 points and thus reduce your cost basis to 27 from 30 [27 (stock price) – 3 (option premium)]. If the stock continued to rise and was above 45 at expiration, it would be called away, which would mean a 66 percent gain for your origi-nal investment [45 (strike price) – 27 (cost basis)/27 (cost basis)].

However, if the stock began to drop, your follow-up action would be to sell the stock and buy back the option for less than what you originally sold it for. For example, if ABC dropped approximately 10 percent (or 4 points) from 42 to 38 over a couple of months, some of the time value would have diminished from the 45 call option that you had sold. It may now be worth 1. At this point, you may be less optimistic about ABC Corporation. Because you had sold the 6-month call for 3 points and it is now worth 1 point, you have pro-tected some of the profit. Had you done nothing, you would have lost 4 points of your profits and, by selling the 45 call, given your-self 3 points of downside protection. In this scenario, you gave up 2 points' profit as compared to 4 points had you taken no action.

HEDGING A SHORT SALE

In Chapter One, we defined a *short sale* as a bearish strategy in which the investor has borrowed a stock to sell, with the hope of buying it back at a later date at a lower price. To hedge this position, the investor could purchase a call on the same underlying stock. The loss would then be limited only to the amount of an at-the-money call premium. At the same time, the investor's profit would come to the amount of decline in the stock less the cost of the call.

For example, suppose IBM stock is selling at $150 per share and a 3-month at-the-money call is selling for 12 points, or $1,200. The investor sells short IBM stock at $150 a share, anticipating that it may be purchased later at a considerably lower price. The investor's risk is that IBM may climb above $150 a share. To limit the potential loss, the investor could buy a call with a striking price of 150 for a premium of $1,200. Regardless of how high the stock rose, the investor would have the right to buy it back at $150 a share. If IBM rose 20 percent, or 30 points, the investor would incur a loss of $1,200—the call's premium—compared to a $3,000 loss had the position not been hedged. Conversely, if IBM dropped in price 20 percent, or 30 points, the investor's profit would be $3,000 less the cost of the option ($3,000 – $1,200) = $1,800).

CONCLUSION

In this chapter, we have discussed a number of situations in which you may sell call options on a common stock. It may be a situation in which you are buying the stock and selling a call simultaneously or perhaps one in which you are selling a call option on stock that you have previously owned. In either case, you can take some follow-up action. If the stock drops, you can roll down, which will give you additional income. If the stock rises, you may elect to roll up, which will allow you to raise the price at which you had originally contracted to relinquish the stock. The point to keep in mind is that you may stick with your original objectives or modify them if there is any significant movement in the stock price.

Chapter
Four

SIMPLE PUT OPTION STRATEGIES

PURCHASE OF PUT OPTIONS

Recall that a put option gives the purchaser the right to sell a stock at a predetermined price—the striking price—between the date of purchase and the option's expiration date. A put option is purchased with the hope that the underlying security will decrease in value. Usually the put option's price increases as the underlying security's price drops.

The purchase of put options is considered a bearish strategy and is used to obtain greater leverage while limiting the investor's loss. It is a purely speculative activity, because the put option is a depleting asset—that is, its value diminishes over time if the underlying stock increases in value or does nothing.

PUT OPTION PURCHASE VERSUS STOCK SHORT SALE The put option purchaser has the same objectives as the short seller. Recall that a *short sale* is defined as the sale of common stock not owned by the seller with the expectation that it may be purchased back at a lower price. Unlike the short seller, however, the put buyer can limit the extent of potential loss by the amount of the premium. Also, the put buyer is not subject to the margin requirements and rules by which the short seller must abide. On the other hand, the short

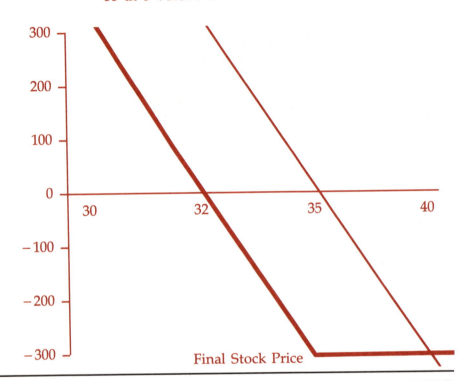

**Exhibit 4-1
Purchase of At-the-Money Put with a Striking Price of 35 at 3 versus Stock Short Sale**

seller is not under the same time constraints as the put option purchaser. For the put buyer, the stock must fall during the option's life.

Exhibit 4-1 compares the purchase of an at-the-money put option with a striking price of 35 and a short sale of the stock at 35. (In the exhibits that follow, the thin line represents stock purchase or short sale and the thick line represents option strategy.) As you can see, the loss on the put is limited to the put's purchase price of $300, which is significantly less than the unlimited potential loss to which the short seller is exposed. In addition, the put clearly provides greater leverage, since the purchaser has a large profit potential while committing much less money than the short seller.

Now let us look at a real-life situation. Suppose you think that retail sales will be sluggish. Thus, you want to speculate that K-Mart

Simple Put Option Strategies

is going to have lower than expected earnings for the quarter and, hence, that the stock price will decline in value. You observe that K-Mart common stock is trading at $50 a share and the put options are priced as follows:

K-Mart 6-month 45, 2 points
K-Mart 6-month 50, 4 points
K-mart 6-month 55, 6 points

A 6-month at-the-money put is selling at 4 points, or $400 for the right to sell 100 shares of K-Mart at 50.

Now suppose that your retail sales scenario proves correct and K-Mart reports lower than expected earnings. In just a few months, K-Mart stock has declined 5 points to 45, meaning a 10 percent gain (5 points profit/50 short stock) for the stock short seller. At the same time, the put price has increased from 4 to 7 (5 points intrinsic value + 2 points time value) for a gain of 75 percent over the same time period [3-point increase in option/4 (option purchase price)]. The reason the put option increased is that your right to sell K-Mart at $50 a share must be worth at least 5 points if K-Mart is now selling at $45 a share. However, there is still some time value remaining in the premium, which is why your 50 put option is worth 7 points. As an investor in this put option, you could sell it in the options market to realize your gain. Had you held 100 shares of K-Mart, you could exercise your right to sell them at $50 per share. This is, however, a separate topic, which we will discuss later in the chapter.

If your retail sales scenario proves incorrect and you shorted 100 shares of K-Mart at 50, your risk theoretically will be unlimited because K-Mart could rise, possibly doubling or even tripling in value. The point to keep in mind is that if you want to speculate on a quick downturn, purchasing a put option may meet your objectives more directly and limit your downside risk by the amount of the put option—in this scenario, $400 versus an unlimited amount.

WHICH TYPE OF OPTION TO PURCHASE? In Chapter Three, we discussed the choice between the purchase of in-the-money, at-the-money, or out-of-the-money calls. The same type of analysis is needed when deciding which put option to purchase. For example, if you expect a major drop in the price of a stock within a relatively short time period, the purchase of the nearest-term at-the-money put option may best meet your objectives.

As in the case of call options, the dollar price should not be the sole factor in your choice of which put option to purchase. The chief consideration is that even though an out-of-the-money put option may provide you with the greatest amount of leverage, it also gives you a greater chance of losing all your money. In addition, if the stock drops only moderately, the in-the-money put option may outperform the out-of-the-money option.

Returning to the K-Mart example, it is clear that had you purchased the out-of-the-money 45 put option at 2, you would have lost the entire investment unless K-Mart stock dropped to 43 during the option's life. In contrast, had you bought the in-the-money 55 put at 6, all you would need to make a profit is for the stock to drop below 49. In this example, you have more dollars at risk by purchasing the in-the-money put option versus the out-of-the-money put option, which is why you must assess the amount of dollar exposure you are willing to assume in any put option purchase decision.

TIME FACTORS The next decision to be made when buying a put option is whether to purchase a 3-, 6-, or 9-month option. Many people purchase the nearest-term out-of-the-money put option simply because it is the cheapest. However, if the stock does not drop within a relatively short period, you will lose the entire investment. Your decision should be based on how quickly you think the underlying stock will decrease in value.

If you are not confident that the decrease will take place in the very near term, you should attempt to purchase the next-furthest-out call option in order to minimize your risk. However, in making this decision it is important to remember that if the stock stays stagnant, the put option will maintain its time value on a consistent basis up until the last six weeks prior to expiration. This is when you will see the quickest deterioration in the option's time value.

PUT OPTION DELTAS In Chapter Two, we discussed how an option's delta measures how much the option will move relative

Simple Put Option Strategies

to the near-term movement of the underlying stock. We also noted that calls have a positive and puts a negative relationship with the underlying stock's price. Hence, put option deltas will be negative. The deeper in-the-money the put option is, the closer to -1 the delta will be. Note too that as time value erodes, so does the option's delta if the underlying stock price remains unchanged. As mentioned in Chapter Three, a delta on a particular stock option can be obtained from a variety of services, including brokers.

As in the case of calls, deltas are an excellent tool to use when deciding which put option to purchase. For example, suppose XYZ stock is trading at 25. The 3-month 25 put option might have a delta of $-.50$ and the 3-month 20 put option a delta of $-.25$. If the stock drops 1 point, the 25 put option will probably increase by one-half of a point and the 20 put option by one-quarter of a point. If you want to purchase a put option that will mimic the stock price movement, you should choose the option that is closest to -1.

PUT OPTIONS AS INSURANCE

PURCHASE OF STOCK AND PUT OPTION SIMULTANEOUSLY

A put option may be seen as a type of insurance when it is purchased simultaneously with a stock. By purchasing the put in conjunction with the stock, you establish a minimum selling price for the stock. Remember that the put purchaser owns the right to sell a stock at a predetermined price. Thus, by purchasing a put and a stock simultaneously, you will limit your loss to the stock price minus the put option's striking price plus the option's premium. If the stock rises, your profit will decrease only by the cost of the put.

In order to fully understand this concept, let us take a look at a realistic scenario. You are bullish on Chrysler Corporation. Chrysler common stock is trading at $35 a share, and the put options are priced as follows:

Chrysler 6-month 30 put, 1 point
Chrysler 6-month 35 put, 3 points
Chrysler 6-month 40 put, 7 points

Since you are bullish on Chrysler, you purchase 100 shares at $35. On the same day, you buy a 6-month at-the-money put for 3 points, or $300. Now your cost basis is $38 [35 (stock price) + 3 (put option price)] a share, but the most you can lose is 3 points because you own the right to sell your stock at $35 a share. If Chrysler rises 20 percent and is trading at 42 at expiration, the 35 put option will expire worthless. The right to sell Chrysler at 35 cannot be worth much if Chrysler is trading at 42 in the marketplace. At this point, you will have realized a $300 loss on the put but also a $700 gain on your stock position for a net gain of $400. If the stock had risen to 42 before expiration, you might have been able to sell the put in the option market for some time value. If Chrysler had declined 20 percent and was trading at 28 at expiration, you could exercise your put option and sell your 100 shares of Chrysler for $35 a share. Your net loss would be the $300 you paid for the option as opposed to $700 had you done nothing.

In this scenario, another alternative would be to sell the put for a profit and hold your stock if you still remain bullish on Chrysler. Here the 6-month 35 put will be worth at least $700 if the underlying stock is trading at 28. Thus, you will have a profit on the put option of at least $400 [700 (current put option price) – 300 (purchase price on put option)]. If Chrysler is unchanged at expiration, the put will expire worthless. However, the put will have acted as term insurance against a decline in the value of Chrysler common stock.

Exhibits 4-2, 4-3, and 4-4 compare the purchase of at-the-money, out-of-the-money, and in-the-money put options, respectively, in conjunction with the purchase of the common stock. As you can see, the put options that are further in-the-money offer you the most protection against a drop in the stock, but they also cost the most.

PURCHASE OF A PUT OPTION WITH AN EXISTING PROFIT ON THE STOCK Purchasing put options on a stock with an existing profit is another way of using put options as insurance. Suppose you have bought 100 shares of Exxon at $50 a share. Over the following year, oil prices stabilize and Exxon records better than expected earnings. As a result, the stock runs up 50 percent (25/50) to $75 a share. As an investor in Exxon, you are concerned that unstable oil prices may negatively impact oil stocks. At this point, you

Simple Put Option Strategies

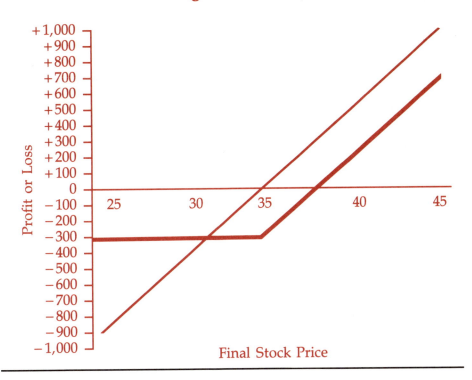

**Exhibit 4-2
Buy Stock at 35 or $3,500; Buy At-the-Money Put
with a Striking Price of 35 at 3 or $300**

may elect to buy a put on Exxon to protect your gain in the long stock position. Remember that the put purchaser owns the right to sell his or her shares of stock at a predetermined price up to and including the expiration date.

In this scenario, Exxon is at 75 and the 6-month put options are priced as follows:

Exxon 6-month 70 put, 2 points
Exxon 6-month 75 put, 6 points
Exxon 6-month 80 put, 10 points

Although you continue to be bullish on Exxon's long-term prospects, you want to protect your capital gains. The purchase of the 6-month at-the-money put with a striking price of 75 for a premium

Exhibit 4-3
Buy Stock at 35 or $3,500; Buy Out-of-the-Money Put with a Striking Price of 30 at 1 or $100

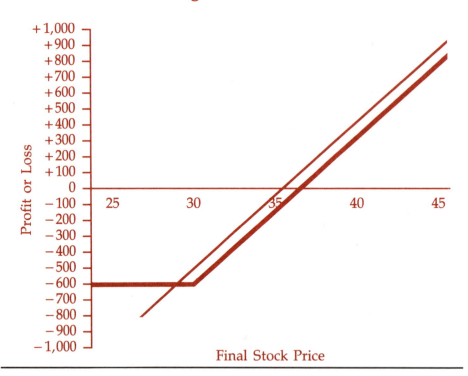

of 6 points, or $600, will give you the right to sell Exxon at $75 a share. Thus, your loss will be limited to the option's cost. You may continue to realize gains if the stock keeps rising; however, any such gains will be reduced by the purchase price of the put.

Given this Exxon example, let us see what the net result on the position will be when the stock rises, declines, and remains unchanged.

If Exxon rises to 93, or 25 percent, you will have participated in the additional gain in your long stock position. The put will drop in value as the stock continues to rise and finally expire worthless, but it will have fulfilled the role of term insurance. You could have limited your loss on the put by selling it in the options market prior to expiration for whatever time value remained.

Simple Put Option Strategies

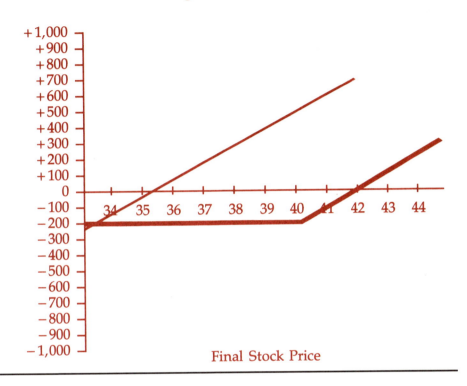

Exhibit 4-4
Buy Stock at 35 or $3,500; Buy In-the-Money Put with a Striking Price of 40 at 7 or $700

If Exxon declines 25 percent, or 18.75 points, to 56.25, you can exercise your put and thus sell your stock for the striking price of $75 a share. Your profit will be the striking price (75) minus the original cost (50) plus the option premium (6). If you continue to remain bullish on Exxon, you can sell the put option for a profit and continue to hold the common stock. In this scenario the put will be worth at least 18.75 points, or the difference between the current market price and the option's striking price.

If Exxon remains unchanged and is $75 at expiration, the put will expire worthless. Again the put will have acted as insurance.

PUT PURCHASE VERSUS STOP-LOSS ORDER In the Exxon example, you may have also considered entering a stop-loss order on the 100 shares of stock. When you enter a stop-loss order, your broker will attempt to sell the stock as soon as it reaches a predetermined price. The advantage of this strategy versus a put purchase is that a stop-loss order has no expiration date; it can be maintained indefinitely. It may also be used on positions of fewer than 100 shares.

A stop-loss order also has disadvantages relative to a put option purchase. In a sharply declining market, the stock may not be sold at all or be sold for less than the desired price. In addition, a stop-loss order does not offer the gains that a put option provides. The put purchaser may exercise the option or sell it for a profit if the underlying stock declines.

USING A PUT OPTION AT YEAR END TO PROTECT GAINS
Another situation in which the purchase of a put on an existing stock may come in handy occurs when you have realized a profit on the stock at year end. In this case, you may want to take the capital gains in the following year. By purchasing a put on the stock with an expiration date in the following year, you will guarantee a selling price.

SELLING PUTS

So far, our discussion has focused on the purchase of puts. Now we will look at the other side of the transaction—selling, or writing, puts.

SELLING PUTS AS A WAY OF ACQUIRING STOCK
Recall that the buyer of a put profits when the underlying stock drops in price. Conversely, the seller of a put profits when the underlying stock increases in value. The seller, or writer, of a put option receives the option premium from the buyer and makes an obligation to buy the stock at the striking price. The seller may, however, cancel the obligation by purchasing a put option in the marketplace with the same striking price and expiration. If the stock is above the striking price at expiration, the put option will expire worthless and the seller will have earned the premium as profit. If the stock is below the striking price, the buyer may exercise the put option and force the seller to purchase the stock at the striking price.

Simple Put Option Strategies

The put writer's objective is to earn premium income or a means of acquiring a common stock at a price lower than the current market price. The writer's cost would be the striking price minus the premium received. Although the put writer may expect the underlying stock to increase in value, he or she should be prepared to acquire the stock at the predetermined striking price. Thus, one should sell puts only on stock on which one is fundamentally bullish.

MARGIN REQUIREMENTS Before examining some specific examples of put writing, let us look at the margin requirements involved.

Under the current requirements, an investor who is short a put must post 20 percent of the value of the underlying stock plus the put's premium less the amount out-of-the-money, with a minimum of $2,000. This may be in the form of cash or double the margin requirement in the case of marginable stock, Treasury securities, and municipal bonds. These margin requirements insure that there will be funds available in the event the stock is put to the investor.

The stringency of margin requirements may vary among brokerage firms. In all cases, however, the requirements must meet the minimum standards set by the Securities and Exchange Commission. For example, if you sold 5 out-of-the-money puts on K-Mart and K-Mart stock was trading at $50 a share and the out-of-the-money 45 put was trading at 2 points, or $200, the margin requirements would be as follows:

20% of K-Mart ($50 × 500 = 25,000)	$5,000
Minus out-of-the-money ($500 × 5 options)	(2,500)
Plus premium	1,000
Margin deposit required	$3,500

An alternative would be to deposit double this amount, or $7,000, in marginable securities. This probably would be a more desirable alternative, since you would be able to keep any interest or dividends accrued by these securities and the cash in a margin account earns no interest. (Note: This situation is given for illustrative purposes only. Be sure to consult your broker for specific margin requirements.)

CHOICE OF PUT OPTION TO WRITE In order to better understand the put-writing strategy, let us look at a realistic situation. Suppose Sears, Roebuck is trading at $40 a share and the put options are priced as follows:

Sears 6-month 35 call, 1 point
Sears 6-month 40 call, 3 points
Sears 6-month 45 call, 7 points

If you are bullish on Sears, you may want to consider selling a 6-month at-the-money put for $3 premium. This will obligate you to purchase 100 shares of Sears at $40 a share within the next 6 months. If the stock is above 40 at expiration, the option will expire worthless. Thus, you will have earned 3 points, or $300. If Sears is trading below $40 per share at expiration, the put option will most likely be exercised and you will have to purchase 100 shares at $40 per share. Thus, your cost basis will be $37 [40 (striking price) − 3 (option premium)]. If Sears is below $37 a share, you will have realized a paper loss. If Sears is unchanged at expiration, the put option will most likely expire worthless. Thus, you will realize a gain of 3 points, or $300.

If you sell an out-of-the-money 35 put, you will receive 1 point. However, you will be taking less risk than an at-the-money or in-the-money put writer. The only time you would sell a deep-in-the-money put would be when the time value was greater than the at-the-money put or you thought there was going to be a substantial rise in the price of the stock.

Exhibits 4-5, 4-6, and 4-7 (pages 83-85) illustrate the selling of an at-the-money put, an out-of-the-money put, and an in-the-money put, respectively. Worksheet 4-1 (page 87) is a sample worksheet for use in establishing and following your put option writing. Worksheet 4-2 (page 88) incorporates data from our Sears, Roebuck example.

In summary, selling puts can be an excellent way to buy stock below current market prices and get paid for it. You can compare this strategy to putting in a good-till-cancelled order below the market and receiving cash up front.

PUT WRITING VERSUS COVERED CALL WRITING In order to better understand the philosophy of selling puts, let us compare

Simple Put Option Strategies

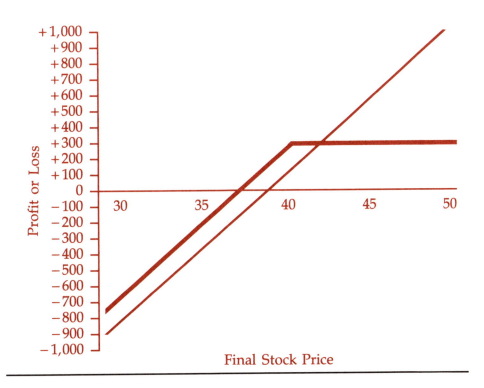

**Exhibit 4-5
Sell At-the-Money Put with a Striking Price of
40 at 3 or $300**

it to a covered call write on the same underlying stock. Assume the following information:

Sears = 40

April 40 call = 5
April 40 put = 4

Put Seller	*Covered Call Writer*	
Sell 1 Apr 40 @ + 400	Buy 100 S @ 40	$4,000
+ ($2,000 cash or	Sell 1 Apr 40 call @ 5	(500)
Marginable securities)	Cash required	$3,500

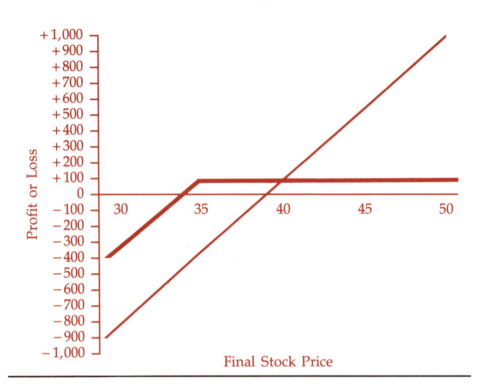

**Exhibit 4-6
Sell Out-of-the-Money Put with a Striking Price of 35 at 1 or $100**

Remember that a covered call writer purchases stock and sells calls against it, thus making an obligation to sell the stock at the striking price. In this example, the covered call writer buys 100 shares of Sears at $40 a share and sells 1 call option with a striking price of 40 for a premium of 5 points, or $500; this provides 5 points of downside protection and 5 points of upside potential. The put seller sells 1 put with a striking price of 40 for 4 points, or $400; this creates the obligation to purchase 100 shares of Sears if it is below $40 a share at expiration. The cost to the covered writer is $3,500 [100 shares of Sears @ 40 – 5 (call option premium)], while the put seller needs only collateral. The put seller may invest the difference in some

Simple Put Option Strategies

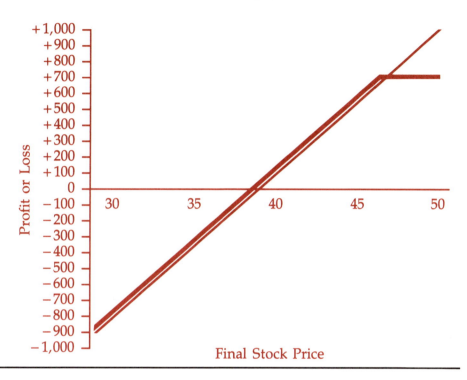

**Exhibit 4-7
Sell In-the-Money Put with a Striking Price of
45 at 7 or $700**

other fixed-income instrument, while the covered call writer will receive dividends from the stock.

Stock Increases 20% to $48 at Expiration:

Short put expires + 400		Stock called @ 40	$4,000
		Original investment	3,500
Gain	$400	Gain	$ 500

With the stock up 20 percent or at $48 at expiration, the covered writer delivers the 100 shares of Sears at 40 for a gain of $500. The short put expires worthless, and the put writer keeps the $400 premium as profit.

Stock Decreases 20% to $32 at Expiration:

Purchase short put	@ 8	Stock down 8 points	$(800)
Originally sold	@ 4	Call premium received	500
Loss	(400)	Loss	$(300)

On the downside, the put writer has a breakeven at 36 (40 strike price – 4 put option premium) and the covered call writer a breakeven at 35 (40 stock purchase price – 5 call option premium). The covered call writer however, has the luxury of being able to hold on to the stock to recoup some or all of the loss if the stock rallies.

In summary, these are both bullish positions. The main difference is that the covered call writer must come up with cash to carry out the strategy, while the uncovered put writer may use his or her portfolio as collateral to establish the position.

Worksheet 4-1
Sample Selling (Writing) Put Option Worksheet

Common stock _____ Current price _____

Put option _____ _____ _____
month   striking   premium
price

Days until expiration _____

A. Initial Position

(1) Sell _____ puts @ _____ $ _____
\#   premium

(2) Less commission   – _____

(3) Net proceeds   = $ _____

(4) Collateral required _____
(see margin requirements)

B. Result of Position If Put Expires
(Occurs If Stock Is above Striking Price)

(5) Profit is equal to (3)   _____

Simple Put Option Strategies

C. Resulting Cost Basis of Stock Position If Puts Are Exercised (Occurs If Stock Is below Striking Price)

(6) Buy _____ shares of _____ @ striking price   _____
          #   stock

(7) Plus commissions   + _____

(8) Gross cost of shares   _____

(9) Net cost of shares [(8) − (3)]   _____

(10) Net cost per share [(9) ÷ (number of shares)]   _____

Worksheet 4-2
Selling (Writing) Put Option Worksheet for Sears

Common stock **Sears** Current price **40**

Put option **June** **40** **3**
         month   striking premium
                 price

Days until expiration **182**

A. Initial Position

(1) Sell **1** puts @ **3** $ **300**
      #   premium

(2) Less commission   − **N/A**

(3) Net proceeds   = $ **300**

(4) Collateral required **2,000**
    (see margin requirements)

B. Result of Position If Put Expires (Occurs If Stock Is above Striking Price)

(5) Profit is equal to (3)   **300**

C. Resulting Cost Basis of Stock If Puts Are Exercised (Occurs If Stock Is below Striking Price)

(6) Buy __100__ shares of __Sears__ @ striking price # · stock	$	__4,000__
(7) Plus commissions	+	__N/A__
(8) Gross cost of shares		__4,000__
(9) Net cost of shares [(8) − (3)]		__3,700__
(10) Net cost per share [(9) ÷ (number of shares)]		__37__

CONCLUSION

In this chapter, we discussed some basic put strategies that can help you achieve some bullish and some bearish objectives. These fundamental strategies, along with the basic call strategies that we explored in Chapter Three, will serve as a foundation for the more advanced strategies to be discussed in the following chapters.

Chapter Five

BASIC SPREADS

DEFINITION OF SPREAD

The option strategies discussed in the preceding chapters are relatively simple. They use either long or short positions in options to achieve the desired objective. However, such positions are associated with a great deal of risk. In this chapter, we introduce the concept of combining long and short option positions to create an overall position with limited risk. Such a limited-risk position is called a *spread*.

In general, a spread may be defined as the simultaneous purchase and sale of options that have the same underlying security and are of the same class but of different series. By this definition, spreads are composed of either puts or calls that differ in either striking price or time to maturity. Positions that employ call options with put options are known as *combinations* and will be discussed in Chapter Six. In this chapter, we will examine three types of spreads: the bull spread, the bear spread, and the time spread.

BULL SPREAD

The *bull spread* is used when one wants to profit from a generally rising market while maintaining a relatively low level of risk. The simplest way to accomplish this is to purchase an at-the-money call option and sell an out-of-the-money call option. In a bull spread, both call options have the same time to maturity but different striking prices.

UNDERLYING LOGIC   The logic behind the bull spread strategy entails taking a long position in the option that will have the greater price appreciation if the market rises. The cost of the long position is reduced by the amount received from the sale of the call option when the short position is established. If one is absolutely certain that the market will rise dramatically, one should purchase call options.

A simple long position in call options has unlimited profit potential but creates the risk of losing the entire amount paid for the options if the market fails to rise as anticipated. A bull spread is less risky than a simple long call option position because the cost of its long position is reduced by the amount of revenue generated by its short option position. However, the spread's profit is much lower than that of the long call option's position. In general, the bull spread's maximum profit potential is equal to the difference between the call options' striking prices less the spread's total cost.

ILLUSTRATIVE BULL SPREAD: FORD MOTOR COMPANY
Exhibit 5-1 shows the behavior of a Ford March 50–60 bull spread over time. The line labeled ''T = 0'' shows the spread's profit or loss at maturity for Ford Motor Company's stock prices ranging from $40 to $80 per share. The line labeled ''T>0'' shows the spread's profit or loss prior to the call options' expiration. Note that when the spread is showing a profit prior to maturity, time becomes an ally for the investor since the profit increases as maturity, T = 0, approaches. Conversely, if the spread is posting a loss prior to expiration, time is working against the investor. However, as the graph shows, the greatest loss the investor can incur is equal to the cost of the spread—in this case, $400.

BACKGROUND   The behavior of Ford's common stock and call option prices between December 1985 and March 1986 provides a good example of conditions favorable for a bull spread. Beginning

Basic Spreads

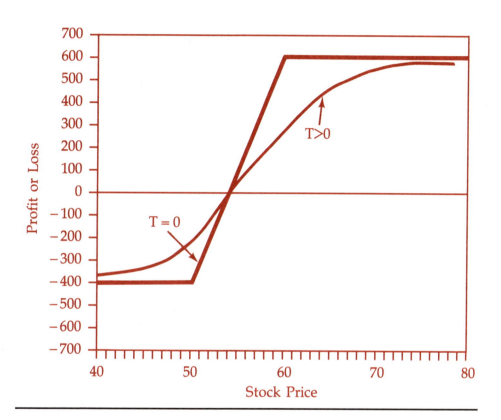

**Exhibit 5-1
Ford Bull Spread
Buy March 50 Call, Sell March 60 Call**

in 1984, the effects of Ford's internal reorganization and commitment to excellence were becoming very evident. Ford had earned record profits and increased its market share during this time period. This success continued in 1985 with a further increase in market share accompanied by another three quarters of large profits. At the beginning of December 1985, Ford's share price stood at 53 3/8, with the March 50 call option trading at 4 3/4 and the March 60 call option trading at 13/16. Given the recent increases in market share and quarterly profits, the company's future seemed quite bright. Thus, the situation was ideal for the creation of a bull spread that would allow a

94   Chapter 5

conservative investor to take part in the anticipated increase in Ford's price while limiting the riskiness of the position. On December 2, 1985, an investor could have created a bull spread in Ford call options by purchasing a March 50 call option for 4¾, or $475, and selling a March 60 call option for ¹³⁄₁₆, or $81.25, for a net cost of 3¹⁵⁄₁₆, or $393.75.

In the following weeks, the prices of Ford's shares and call options began to rise. These price increases were caused in part by a *Fortune* cover story in December 1985 that lavishly praised Ford's cost control measures and the dramatic changes instituted in the design and production of Ford's products. The market responded by bidding up the price of Ford shares to 57⅞, the price of the March 50 call option to 8⅛, and the price of the March 60 call to 1¾ on December 30. These call option prices translated into a value of 6⅜, or $637.50, for the Ford March 50–60 bull spread, computed by taking the value of the long position, 8⅛ for the March 50 call option, and subtracting the value of the short position, 1¾ for the March 60 call option.

Ford's share price and call option prices continued to rise in January and February of 1986. On February 10, Ford's common stock closed at 66¼, the March 50 call option at 16⅝, the March 60 call option at 6⅞, and the March 65 call option at 4¾. Given these prices, the value of the March 50–60 bull spread was 9¾ (16⅝ – 6⅞), or $975.

ROLLING UP   With approximately six weeks left until the March options' expiration, investors had to make a decision. There were three alternatives:

1. Do nothing and leave the spread intact.
2. Close out the position and take a $581.25 profit [$975 (current value) – $393.75 (original cost)].
3. Use the existing spread's profits to create another spread by rolling up. An investor *rolls up* from one call option position to another by closing out the position with the lower striking price and opening a position with a higher striking price.

Had the first alternative—doing nothing—been chosen, the current profit of 5¹³⁄₁₆ points, or $581.25, would have been jeopardized. Indeed, an investor who was long the bull spread was exposing the position's value to an accelerating time decay during the six weeks remaining until the spread's maturity. Any further profit for this

Basic Spreads

spread would have to have been provided by an increase in Ford's stock price that was large enough to outweigh the effects of the time decay. Given that the price of Ford's common stock had already risen by approximately 13 points since the spread was created, one had to wonder whether Ford's stock price could have continued its strong showing for another six weeks. Thus, the first alternative seemed to be needlessly risky for the prudent investor.

The second alternative—closing the position and taking the profits— would have circumvented the problem of unnecessarily exposing the position to the rapid time decay. However, the investor would have forsaken the profit potential associated with any further increase in Ford's stock price. With six weeks remaining in the spread's life, the investor's goal should have been to profit from any further increases in Ford's stock price while minimizing the effects of time decay.

The third alternative—rolling up—would have provided the investor with a strategy for achieving this goal. In this situation, the investor could have accomplished the roll-up from the Ford March 50–60 spread to the Ford March 60–65 spread via the following steps.

First, the March 50–60 bull spread had to be closed out by selling the March 50 call option for $16\frac{5}{8}$ points and purchasing a March 60 call option for $6\frac{7}{8}$ points for a cash inflow of $9\frac{3}{4}$ points, or $975. The difference between this cash inflow and the March 50–60 spread's original cost of $393.75 would have been a profit of $5\frac{13}{16}$ points, or $581.25.

Second, the March 60–65 bull spread had to be established by purchasing a March 60 call option for $6\frac{7}{8}$ points and selling a March 65 call option for $4\frac{3}{4}$ points for a net cost of $2\frac{1}{8}$ points, or $212.50. Note that the cost of the March 60–65 spread would have been more than covered by the profits generated from the March 50–60 spread. Thus, after rolling up the investor could have pocketed the $368.75 difference between the profits of the March 50–60 spread and the cost of the March 60–65 spread ($581.25 − $212.50) while maintaining a position in the market that would permit profiting from any further increases in the price of Ford common stock.

The only unappealing aspect of this strategy is that the investor would have been unable to pocket an amount equal to the cost of the March 50–60 spread, $393.75, when rolling up. Ideally there

96   Chapter 5

should be enough profit available to cover the cost of the new spread as well as that of the original. In this case, the $368.75 remaining after rolling up into the March 60–65 spread would have been $25 less than the cost of the original March 50–60 spread. Thus, had the price of Ford's stock dropped to less than 60 by expiration, the investor would have stood to lose a total of $25 plus commissions.

During the next six weeks, Ford's share price rose steadily. The share price increase was accompanied by a rise in the options' values. Hence, on March 17, four days before expiration, Ford's common stock had reached a level of $72\frac{5}{8}$, the March 50 call option was at $22\frac{5}{8}$, the March 60 call option was at $12\frac{3}{4}$, and the March 65 call option had a price of $7\frac{7}{8}$. Given these prices, the value of the March 50–60 bull spread was $9\frac{7}{8}$, or $987.50, while the March 60–65 bull spread was $4\frac{7}{8}$, or $487.50. Since this was Monday of the expiration week, it was time for conservative investors to close out their positions.

If an investor had established the Ford March 50–60 bull spread in December and then left it intact until expiration week, the spread would have earned a profit of $5\frac{15}{16}$ points, or $593.75—that is, the $987.50 value at liquidation minus the original cost of $393.75. An impressive gain—but one that is virtually equal to the profit that could have been taken on February 10, six weeks prior to maturity, even though the price of Ford's common stock rose approximately six points between February 2 and March 17. This illustrates the powerful effect of time decay on the position's value and emphasizes the advantage of rolling up to protect the bull spread's gains.

The March 17 prices for Ford's common stock and call options translate into a value of $4\frac{7}{8}$ points, or $487.60, for the March 60–65 bull spread: $12\frac{3}{4}$ points for the long position in the March 60 call option minus $7\frac{7}{8}$ points for the short position in the March 65 call option. The investor who had rolled up from the March 50–60 to the March 60–65 bull spread could have closed the latter and captured the entire $487.60, since that spread would have been funded by the profits from the March 50–60 spread. However, this would have been only part of the total profit generated by the rolling-up strategy. Recall that the investor could have pocketed $3\frac{11}{16}$ points, or $368.75, when the March 60–65 bull spread was created. Thus, the total profit from this strategy would have been $856.35, or

Basic Spreads

approximately 8 9/16 points: $487.60 profit at liquidation of the March 60–65 spread plus $368.75 profit from the March 50–60 spread. This clearly would have been a better outcome than the result of simply leaving the March 50–60 spread six weeks prior to expiration.

SAMPLE WORKSHEETS Worksheets 5-1 and 5-2 present the computations for the Ford bull spread and subsequent roll-up, respectively. Both worksheets begin with sections that organize the stock and call option data in terms of current market prices, maturities, and striking prices. Lines 1 through 5 are identical in both worksheets; they provide the investor with the net cost of the initial position. Worksheet 5-1 is completed with the liquidation data and the profit-or-loss computations. In Worksheet 5-2, the roll-up section documents the transition from the Ford March 50–60 bull spread to the Ford March 60–65 bull spread. The value for the roll-up cash flow is derived by subtracting the cost of purchasing the options (line 8) from the total amount of revenue generated by the sale of the options (line 6 plus line 10). Finally, note that on line 8 the investor is selling both options in tandem rather than separately. This will save commissions and should be done whenever possible.

BEAR SPREAD

The *bear spread* is used when one wants to profit from a declining market while maintaining a relatively low level of risk. The easiest way to accomplish this is by purchasing an at-the-money put option and selling an out-of-the-money put option. In a bear spread, both put options have the same time to maturity but different striking prices.

UNDERLYING LOGIC As in the case of the bull spread, the logic behind the bear spread consists of establishing a long position in the option that will result in the greater gain if the stock moves as anticipated. Also as in the bull spread, the revenue generated by the short position is used to offset part of the long position's cost. If the investor is positive that the market is going to fall, he or she should purchase put options.

Worksheet 5-1
Bull Spread Purchase Worksheet

A. Position Data

Underlying stock __Ford__   Current price __$53\frac{3}{8}$__

Days until option expiration __86__

Options' maturity month __March__

Low striking price __50__   High striking price __60__

Low strike option intrinsic value __$3\frac{3}{8}$__

Low strike option time value __$1\frac{3}{8}$__

Low strike option premium __$4\frac{3}{4}$__

High strike option intrinsic value __0__

High strike option time value __$\frac{13}{16}$__

High strike option premium __$\frac{13}{16}$__

B. Initial Position

(1) Sell __1__ high strike options @ __$\frac{13}{16}$__ for $ __81.25__

(2) Less commissions $ __N/A__

(3) Buy __1__ low strike options @ __$4\frac{3}{4}$__ for $ __475.00__

(4) Plus commissions $ __N/A__

(5) Net cost $ __393.75__

C. Position Profit or Loss

The position's maximum loss will equal the net cost (5) and will occur if both the options are out-of-the-money when they expire. Under these conditions, neither option will have any intrinsic value and both will expire worthless.

Stock price at liquidation __$72\frac{5}{8}$__

Days until option expiration __4__

Options' maturity month __March__

Low striking price __50__   High striking price __60__

Low strike option intrinsic value $22\frac{5}{8}$

Low strike option time value 0

Low strike option premium $\qquad$ $22\frac{5}{8}$

High stike option intrinsic value $12\frac{5}{8}$

High strike option time value $\frac{1}{8}$

High strike option premium $\qquad$ $12\frac{3}{4}$

(6) Buy 1 high strike options @ $12\frac{3}{4}$ for $ $1,275

(7) Plus commissions $ N/A

(8) Sell 1 low strike options @ $22\frac{5}{8}$ for $ $2,262.50

(9) Less commissions $ N/A

(10) Net revenues $ $987.50

Net profit or loss [(10) – (5)] $ $593.75

Worksheet 5-2
Bull Spread Roll Up Worksheet

A. Initial Position Data

Underlying stock __Ford__   Current price $53\frac{3}{8}$

Days until option expiration __86__

Options' maturity month __March__

Low striking price __50__   High striking price __60__

Low strike option intrinsic value $3\frac{3}{8}$

Low strike option time value $1\frac{3}{8}$

Low strike option premium $\qquad$ $4\frac{3}{4}$

High strike option intrinsic value 0

High strike option time value $\frac{13}{16}$

High strike option premium $\qquad$ $\frac{13}{16}$

(1) Sell 1 high strike options @ $\frac{13}{16}$ for $ $81.25

(2) Less commissions $ N/A

(3) Buy 1 low strike options @ $4\frac{3}{4}$ for $ $475.00

100   Chapter 5

(4) Plus commissions $ ___N/A___

(5) Net cost $ __393.75__

B. Roll-Up Position Data

Underlying stock ___Ford___ Current price ___66¼___

Days until option expiration ___45___

Option premium ___16⅝___ @ striking price ___50___

Option premium ___6⅞___ @ striking price ___60___

Option premium ___4¾___ @ striking price ___65___

(6) Sell ___1___ options strike = ___50___ @ ___16⅝___   for $ __1,662.50__

(7) Less commissions $ ___N/A___

(8) Buy ___2___ options strike = ___60___ @ ___6⅞___   for $ __1,375__

(9) Plus commissions $ ___N/A___

(10) Sell ___1___ options strike = ___65___ @ ___4¾___   for $ __475.00__

(11) Less commissions $ ___N/A___

(12) Roll-up cash flow $ __762.50__

(13) Net cash flow [(12) − (5)] $ __368.75__

C. Total Position Profit or Loss

Stock price at liquidation   __72⅝__

Days until option expiration ___4___

Options' maturity month __March__

Low striking price ___60___ High striking price ___65___

Low strike option intrinsic value ___12⅝___

Low strike option time value ___⅛___

Low strike option premium   __12¾__

High strike option·intrinsic value ___7⅝___

High strike option time value ___¼___

High strike option premium   __7⅞__

(14) Buy __1__ options strike = __65__ @ __7⅞__	for	$	787.50
(15) Plus commissions		$	N/A
(16) Sell __1__ options strike = __60__ @ __12¾__	for	$	1,275
(17) Less commissions		$	N/A
(18) Net revenues		$	487.50
Net profit or loss [(18) + (13)]		$	856.25

While a simple long position in put options has a large profit potential—equal to the striking price minus the position's total cost—it entails the risk of losing the entire amount paid for the options if the market fails to fall as expected. A bear spread is less risky than a simple long put option position, because the cost of the spread's long position is reduced by the amount of revenue generated by its short option position. However, the spread's profit potential is much smaller than that of the long put option's position. In general, the bear spread's maximum profit potential is equal to the difference between the put options' striking prices and the spread's total cost.

ILLUSTRATIVE BEAR SPREAD: AMOCO   Exhibit 5-2 shows the behavior of an Amoco February 60–65 bear spread over time. The line labeled "T = 0" shows the spread's profit or loss at maturity for Amoco's stock prices ranging from $50 to $80 per share. The line labeled "T > 0" shows the bear spread's profit or loss prior to the put options' expiration. When the spread is showing a profit prior to maturity, time becomes an ally for the investor because the profit increases as maturity (T = 0) approaches. On the other hand, if the spread is showing a loss prior to expiration, time is working against the investor. The greatest loss the investor can suffer is equal to the $200 cost of the spread.

BACKGROUND   The situation that prevailed in the international oil market between the autumn of 1985 and the spring of 1986 created conditions that were conducive to bear spreads in some oil sector stocks. At this time, it appeared that OPEC was disintegrating. The Saudi Arabians were unable to forge pricing and production agree-

**Exhibit 5-2
Amoco Bear Spread
Buy February 65 Put, Sell February 60 Put**

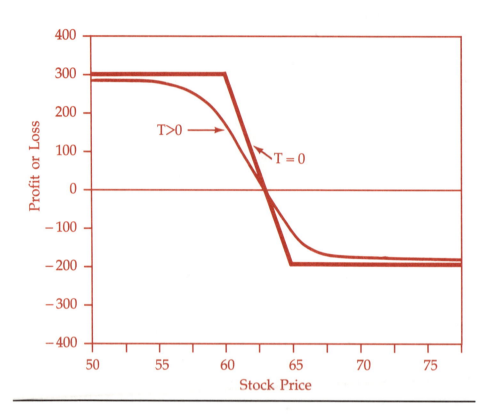

ments within OPEC. Cash-starved OPEC members, such as Nigeria, were attempting to gain market share by cutting prices and boosting production. The chaos within OPEC caused crude-oil prices to plummet in the world market and was deemed responsible for the falling share prices of many oil company stocks.

Amoco was among the oil companies whose shares were adversely affected by the drop in crude-oil prices. On December 9, 1985, the price of Amoco's common stock was 63⅜, down by more than 4 points from its Thanksgiving value of 67¾; the Amoco February 60 put option was at ⅝; and the Amoco February 65 put option had a value of 2½. Given the situation in the international petroleum

Basic Spreads   103

market, it was doubtful that Amoco's share price would recover—indeed, it seemed more likely that it would continue to drop in the near future. However, it was uncertain whether Amoco's share price would fall as rapidly as some analysts were predicting. A bear spread in Amoco put options was a relatively low-risk strategy that offered the conservative investor an opportunity to profit from this situation.

Thus, on December 9 an Amoco February 60–65 bear spread could have been formed by purchasing the February 65 put option for 2½ points and selling the February 60 put option for ⅝ points. The net cost of the spread—$187.50, or 1⅞ points—was the difference between the amount paid for the February 65 put option ($250) and the amount received for the sale of the February 60 put option ($62.50).

There are two things worth noting about this bear spread. First, there was only a 5-point difference between the striking prices. Due to liquidity considerations, it is usually best to form bear spreads with put options that are one striking price apart. Those that are formed with put options that are more than one striking price apart run the risk of having the spread's long put option position go deep in-the-money, which means that the long put option position may be worth exercising. Since market makers will be unwilling to trade this put option if exercise is imminent, there will be virtually no market volume, or liquidity, for the option. Thus, the investor will find it nearly impossible to liquidate the spread at a fair price.

The second noteworthy feature of the Amoco spread is that it was established for less than 2 points, or $200. This is important when one considers commissions, since the spread's maximum profit is equal to the difference between the striking prices and the spread's total cost. If the difference between the spread's long position and short position is too great, there will be very little profit available to the investor after commissions are paid.

In the following weeks, the bear spread's value rose while Amoco's share price continued to fall. On January 17, 1986, Amoco's common stock had a value of 60⅜, the February 55 put option had a price of ⅜, the February 60 put option was at 1⅝, and the value of the February 65 put option was 5. These put option prices implied a value of 3⅜, or $337.50, for the Amoco February 60–65 bear spread: the 5-point value of the February 65 put option long position minus the 1⅝-point value of the February 60 put option short position.

ROLLING DOWN   With five weeks left until the spread's expiration, investors had to make a decision. As in the case of the Ford bull spread, there were three alternatives:

1. Do nothing and leave the spread intact.
2. Close out the position and take a $150 profit [$337.50 (current value) – $187.50 (original cost)].
3. Use the existing spread's profits to create another spread by rolling down. An investor *rolls down* from one put option position to another by closing out the position with the higher striking price and opening a position at a lower striking price.

By choosing the first alternative—doing nothing—the investor would have jeopardized the spread's profit of 1½ points, or $150, by exposing the position's value to an accelerating time decay during the remainder of the spread's life. Thus, the first alternative seemed unnecessarily risky for the conservative investor.

The second alternative—closing the position and taking the profits—would not have exposed the position's profits to rapid time decay. However, by choosing this tactic the investor would have forfeited any profits generated by further decreases in Amoco's stock price. With five weeks remaining in the spread's life, the investor's goal should have been to profit from any subsequent decreases in the price of Amoco stock while minimizing the effects of time decay.

The third alternative—rolling down—offered a strategy with which to achieve this goal. In this situation, the investor would have rolled down from the Amoco February 60–65 to the Amoco February 55–60 bear spread via the following steps.

First, the investor would have closed out the February 60–65 spread by selling the February 65 put option for 5 points and purchasing a February 60 put option at 1⅝ points for a profit of 1½ points, or $150.

Second, the February 55–60 bear spread would have been created by purchasing a February 60 put option for 1⅝ points and selling a February 55 put option for ⅜ points for a net cost of 1¼ points, or $125. Note that the cost of the February 55–60 spread would have been covered by the profits generated by the February 60–65 spread. Thus, after rolling down the investor would have been able to keep the $25 difference between the profits of the February 60–65 bull spread and the cost of the February 55–60 bull spread ($150 – $125) while maintaining a market position that would have profited from any further decline in the price of Amoco common stock.

Like the rolling-up strategy used in the bull spread case, rolling down posed a disadvantage: The investor would have been unable to keep an amount equal to the cost of the February 60–65 spread ($187.50). Here the $25 left for the investor would have been $162.50 short of the amount required for covering the spread. Thus, if the price of Amoco's stock had risen to more than 60 by expiration, the investor would have stood to lose a total of $162.50 plus commissions.

Between January 17 and February 7, Amoco's share price fell steadily to 56¼. This drop was accompanied by an increase in the prices of the February put options. On February 7, the Amoco February 55 put option was at ⅝, the February 60 put option at 4¾, and the February 65 put option at 9½. At these prices, the value of the February 55–60 bear spread was 4⅛ (the difference between the 4¾ value of the long position in the February 60 put option and the ⅝ value of the short position in the February 55 put option) while the February 60–65 bear spread had a value of 4¾ (the 9½ value of the long position in the February 65 put option minus the 4¾ value of the short position in the February 60 put option). Since crude-oil prices appeared to have stabilized, it seemed unlikely that Amoco's share price would suffer further erosion. Thus, it was time for investors to close out their positions.

If an investor had established the Amoco 60–65 bear spread in December and then left it intact until February 7, the spread would have earned a profit of 2⅞ points, or $287.50 ($475 value at liquidation minus the original cost of $187.50). On the other hand, an investor who had rolled down from the February 60–65 bear spread to the February 55–60 bear spread could have closed the latter for a profit equal to the liquidation value of 4⅛ points, since that spread was funded with the profits from the February 60–65 spread. However, this would have been only part of the total profit generated by the rolling-down strategy. Recall that the investor would have been able to keep ¼ points, or $25, when the February 55–60 spread was created. Therefore, the total profit for this strategy would have been 4⅜ points, or $437.50 ($412.50 profit at liquidation of the February

55–60 spread plus the $25 profit from the February 60–65 spread)—again a better outcome than would have resulted from simply leaving the original spread intact.

SAMPLE WORKSHEETS Worksheets 5-3 and 5-4 present the computations for the Amoco bear spread and roll-down, respectively. These are basically the same as the bull spread worksheets, 5-1 and 5-2. As before, both worksheets begin with sections that organize the stock and option data in terms of current market prices, maturities, and striking prices. On both worksheets, lines 1 through 5 are identical and provide the investor with the net cost of the initial position. Worksheet 5-3 contains the liquidation data and profit-or-loss computations. In Worksheet 5-4, the roll-down section documents the transition from the Amoco February 60–65 bear spread to the February 55–60 bear spread. The value for the roll-down cash flow is derived by subtracting the cost of purchasing the options (line 8) from the total amount of revenue generated by their sale (line 6 plus line 10). Finally, on line 8 the investor is selling both put options in one transaction to save commissions.

TIME SPREAD

The *time spread*, or *calender spread*, is used by an investor who is neither bullish nor bearish. The time spread is profitable in flat—that is, unchanging—markets. The spread's profitability results from the accelerating time decay of the option's premium as maturity approaches. Its components are at-the-money options that have identical striking prices but different maturity dates.

Since the options are at-the-money, they have no intrinsic value; their prices are composed entirely of time value. Theoretically an investor can create a time spread from either call options or put options. In the following examples we will use only call options, since they have several advantages over put options, including greater liquidity and larger time value.

UNDERLYING LOGIC When creating a time spread, the investor purchases the longer-maturity at-the-money call option and sells

Basic Spreads

107

Worksheet 5-3
Bear Spread Purchase Worksheet

A. Position Data

Underlying stock **Amoco** Current price **63⅜**

Days until option expiration **52**

Options' maturity month **February**

Low striking price **60** High striking price **65**

Low strike option intrinsic value **0**

Low strike option time value **⅝**

Low strike option premium   **⅝**

High strike option intrinsic value **1⅝**

High strike option time value **⅞**

High strike option premium   **2½**

B. Initial Position

(1) Sell **1** low strike options @ **⅝** for $ **62.50**

(2) Less commissions $ **N/A**

(3) Buy **1** high strike options @ **2½** for $ **250.00**

(4) Plus commissions $ **N/A**

(5) Net cost $ **187.50**

C. Position Profit or Loss

The position's maximum loss will equal the net cost (5) and will occur if both the options are out-of-the-money when they expire. Under these conditions, neither option will have any intrinsic value and both will expire worthless.

Stock price at liquidation   **56¼**

Days until option expiration **14**

Options' maturity month **February**

Low striking price **60** High striking price **65**

Low strike option intrinsic value ___3¾___

Low strike option time value ___1___

Low strike option premium   ___4¾___

High stike option intrinsic value ___8¾___

High strike option time value ___¾___

High strike option premium   ___9½___

(6) Buy ___1___ low strike options @ ___4¾___ for $ ___475.00___

(7) Plus commissions $ ___N/A___

(8) Sell ___1___ high strike options @ ___9½___ for $ ___950.00___

(9) Less commissions $ ___N/A___

(10) Net revenues $ ___475.00___

Net profit or loss [(10) − (5)] $ ___287.50___

Worksheet 5-4
Bear Spread Roll Down Worksheet

A. Initial Position Data

Underlying stock __Amoco__ Current price ___63⅜___

Days until option expiration ___52___

Options' maturity month __February__

Low striking price ___60___ High striking price ___65___

Low strike option intrinsic value ___0___

Low strike option time value ___⅝___

Low strike option premium   ___⅝___

High strike option intrinsic value ___1⅝___

High strike option time value ___⅞___

High strike option premium   ___2½___

(1) Sell ___1___ low strike options @ ___⅝___ for $ ___62.50___

(2) Less commissions $ ___N/A___

(3) Buy ___1___ high strike options @ ___2½___ for $ ___250.00___

Basic Spreads

(4) Plus commissions $ __N/A__

(5) Net cost $ __187.50__

B. Roll-Down Position Data

Underlying stock __Amoco__ Current price __60⅜__

Days until option expiration __35__

Option premium __⅜__ @ striking price __55__

Option premium __1⅝__ @ striking price __60__

Option premium __5__ @ striking price __65__

(6) Sell __1__ options strike = __65__ @ __5__ for $ __500.00__

(7) Less commissions $ __N/A__

(8) Buy __2__ options strike = __60__ @ __1⅝__ for $ __325.00__

(9) Plus commissions $ __N/A__

(10) Sell __1__ options strike = __55__ @ __⅜__ for $ __37.50__

(11) Less commissions $ __N/A__

(12) Roll-down cash flow $ __212.50__

(13) Net cash flow [(12) – (5)] $ __25.00__

C. Total Position Profit or Loss

Stock price at liquidation __56¼__

Days until option expiration __14__

Options' maturity month __February__

Low striking price __55__ High striking price __60__

Low strike option intrinsic value __0__

Low strike option time value __⅝__

Low strike option premium __⅝__

High strike option intrinsic value __3¾__

High strike option time value __1__

High strike option premium __4¾__

(14) Buy __1__ options strike = __55__ @ __⅝__ for	$	__62.50__
(15) Plus commissions	$	__N/A__
(16) Sell __1__ options strike = __60__ @ __4¾__ for	$	__475.00__
(17) Less commissions	$	__N/A__
(18) Net revenues	$	__412.50__
Net profit or loss [(18) + (13)]	$	__437.50__

the nearby at-the-money call option. The spread's cost is the difference between the amount paid for the longer-term call option and the amount received for the shorter-term option. Since the underlying stock's price is expected to remain stable, the logic entails the investor's being long the option that will retain the greater amount of value as time passes and being short the option that will lose the greater amount of value as maturity approaches.

Ideally the investor wants both call options to be at-the-money when the nearby call option matures, because this is where the time spread's maximum profit is earned. In this situation, neither the long nor short call option position will have any intrinsic value. Thus, the spread's short position will expire worthless while the long position will retain most of its original value. The difference between the long position's value and the short position's value therefore will have increased during the time spread's life, which means a profit for the investor.

The time spread's risk is relatively low, since the maximum amount that can be lost is the spread's cost. This will occur if the underlying stock makes a large move such that both call options are either deep in-the-money or deep out-of-the-money at the nearby call option's expiration. In general, when options are far-from-the-money they have virtually no time premium. Thus, the difference between the value of the long call option position and the short call option position will be nearly zero.

If flat, or unchanging, share prices are anticipated, the time spread is a much better strategy for the conservative investor than either call writing or put writing. These simple writing strategies carry enormous amounts of risk for very little profit. In contrast, the time

Basic Spreads 111

spread has a limited level of risk and almost as much profit potential as the option writing strategies in flat markets. In spite of this favorable risk-return relationship, however, some investors would rather receive a cash inflow from writing options than pay a cash outflow from creating a time spread. We feel that the writing strategies are too risky and strongly recommend that the time spread be used when flat markets are anticipated.

Exhibit 5-3 provides an illustration typical of utility stocks. It shows the behavior of a Commonwealth Edison March–June time spread. The line labeled "T = 0" shows the spread's profit or loss at maturity for Edison stock prices ranging from $20 to $40 per share. The line labeled "T>0" shows the spread's profit or loss prior to the call options' expiration. As with bull and bear spreads, time becomes an ally for the investor since the profit increases as maturity (T = 0) approaches. Conversely, if the spread exhibits a loss prior to expiration, time is working against the investor. In this case, the greatest loss the investor can incur is equal to the cost of the spread, $60.

ILLUSTRATIVE TIME SPREAD: FIRESTONE TIRE & RUBBER

BACKGROUND In the last half of 1986, Firestone Tire & Rubber Company seemed to be behaving like a utility. The share price and call option price behavior provided ideal conditions for the creation of time spreads. From 1980 through 1985, Firestone underwent some major changes. Businesses that were unrelated to the automotive industry were sold. Manufacturing plants were closed, and the number of employees was reduced by nearly half. Firestone decided to concentrate on the original equipment tire market and to enter the automobile servicing industry. These changes resulted in a much smaller company and a share price of about $25—more than triple the 1980 share price of $8.

Despite Firestone's great strides over the preceding five years, the company still had much room for improvement in 1986. Given this situation, many analysts did not expect Firestone's share price to make any major moves in the near future. An investor wishing to take advantage of this situation via a low-risk position would have been wise to construct a time spread using Firestone call options.

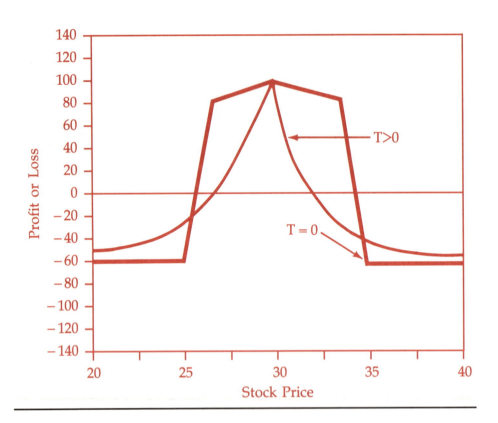

**Exhibit 5-3
Time Spread
Sell March 30 Call, Buy June 30 Call**

On May 29, 1986, the share price of Firestone stock stood at 23⅞, the August 25 call option's price was ¹³⁄₁₆, and the price of the November 25 call option was 1⅛. At this time, an investor could have created a time spread in Firestone call options by purchasing a November 25 call option for 1⅛ points, or $112.50, and selling an August 25 call option for ¹³⁄₁₆, or $81.25, for a net cost of ⁵⁄₁₆, or $31.25. Note that both options were out-of-the-money and that the difference in their values was composed entirely of the difference between their time premiums. Further, the maximum amount the investor could have lost was the spread's cost ($31.25) plus any commissions paid.

Basic Spreads

In the ensuing weeks, Firestone's share price made a series of small, erratic moves, culminating at a level of 25⅛ on July 25, approximately three weeks prior to the August 25 call option's expiration. The value of the August 25 call option had declined to ½ points from its May 29 value of ¹³⁄₁₆; the November 25 call option had increased in value to 1¾ from its earlier value of 1⅛; and the February 25 call option was at 2¼ points. These call option prices translated into a value of 1¼ points, or $125, for the Firestone 25 August–November time spread: the value of the long position (1¾ for the November 25 call option) minus the value of the short position (½ for the August 25 call option). They also indicated that the spread had generated a profit of ¹⁵⁄₁₆ points, or $93.75: the $125 July 25 value minus the $31.25 cost.

The spread's value had risen from ⁵⁄₁₆ to 1¼ because the difference between the prices of the August 25 and November 25 call options had increased. The principal reason for this increase was the time decay's extremely powerful effect on the nearby call option's price. This effect was dramatically illustrated by the fact that the value of the August 25 call—the nearby option—had deteriorated despite the rise in Firestone's share price.

ROLLING FORWARD With only three weeks left until the Firestone time spread's expiration, investors were forced to make a decision. There were three possible courses of action:

1. Do nothing and leave the spread intact.
2. Close out the position and take the $93.75 profit.
3. Use the existing spread's profits to create another spread by rolling forward. An investor *rolls forward* from one time spread to another by closing out the spread with the closer maturity and creating one with a more distant maturity.

Given that there were only three weeks remaining in the spread's life and that the stock and call option prices were at ideal levels, it would have been foolish to risk the time spread's profits until the August 25 call option had matured. Choosing the first alternative—doing nothing—would have subjected the spread's profit of ¹⁵⁄₁₆ points, or $93.75, to the possibility that Firestone's share price would be far different from 25⅛ when the August 25 call option expired.

This would have meant a loss of time premium for the spread and less profit for the investor. Thus, the first alternative seemed needlessly risky for the prudent investor.

The second alternative—closing out the position and taking the profits—would not have exposed the spread's profits to the effects of share price movement. However, the investor would have forfeited any profits generated by an unchanging Firestone share price and a rapidly decaying August 25 call option price. At this point, the investor's goal should have been to create a position that would permit profiting from a relatively stable Firestone share price by capitalizing on the effects of time decay.

The third alternative—rolling forward—offered a strategy for attaining this goal. In this situation, the investor could have rolled forward from the Firestone August–November time spread to the November–February time spread via the following steps.

First, the August–November spread had to be closed out by selling the November 25 call option for 1¾ points and purchasing an August 25 call option for ½ points for a cash inflow of 1¼ points, or $125. The difference between this cash inflow and the August–November spread's original cost of $31.25 would have been a profit of $^{15}/_{16}$ points, or $93.75.

Second, the November–February spread had to be established by purchasing a February 25 call option for 2¼ points and selling a November 25 call option for 1¾ points for a net cost of ½ point, or $50. Observe that the cost of the November–February spread would have been less than the profits generated by the August–November spread. Thus, after rolling forward the investor would have been able to retain the $43.75 difference between the profits of the August–November spread and the cost of the November–February spread ($125 – $50) while maintaining a market position conducive to profiting from a stable Firestone common stock price.

Unlike the case of either the bull or bear spread, the investor would have been able to keep an amount after rolling forward— $43.75—that was $12.50, or ⅛ points, more than the $31.25 cost of the original August–November time spread. Thus, had the price of Ford stock made a big move before the November 25 call option's expiration, the investor would have lost an amount equal to the commission charges.

Basic Spreads 115

During the next three months, Firestone's share price remained quite stable and the value of the November–February time spread appreciated. On October 15, Firestone's common stock was at 25, the November 25 call option was down to $^{15}\!/_{16}$ from its July 25 value of 1¾, and the February 25 call option's value had dropped to $1^{15}\!/_{16}$ from its previous level of 2¼. Given these prices, the value of the November–February spread was 1 point, or $100: the $1^{15}\!/_{16}$-point value of the February 25 call option minus the 1-point value of the November 25 call option. Since many analysts were predicting that Firestone's share value would increase in the near future, it was time for investors to close out the November–February time spread.

The October 15 prices for Firestone's common stock and call options imply a total profit of $1^7\!/_{16}$ points, or $143.75, for the investor who had rolled forward from the August–November spread to the November–February spread. This investor could have closed the November–February spread for a 1-point, or $100, profit since it had been funded by the profits from the August–November spread. However, this would have been only part of the total profit generated by the rolling-forward strategy. Remember that the investor was able to keep $^7\!/_{16}$ points, or $43.75, when the August–November time spread was created. Thus, the total profit from this strategy would have been $1^7\!/_{16}$ points, or $143.75: $100 profit at liquidation of the November–February spread plus $43.75 profit from the August–November spread. As in the bull and bear spread examples, this would have been a much more desirable outcome than would have resulted from simply allowing the August–November spread to expire.

SAMPLE WORKSHEETS Worksheets 5-5 and 5-6 illustrate the computations for the Firestone time spread and subsequent roll-forward, respectively. Each begins with a section that organizes the stock and call option data in terms of current market prices, maturities, and striking prices. Lines 1 through 5 of both worksheets are identical; they provide information on the net cost of the time spread's initial position. Like Worksheets 5-1 and 5-3, Worksheet 5-5 concludes with the liquidation data and profit-or-loss computations. In Worksheet 5-6, the roll-forward section exhibits the transition from the Firestone August–November time spread to the Firestone November–February time spread.

116   Chapter 5

Worksheet 5-5
Time Spread Purchase Worksheet

A. Position Data

Underlying stock **Firestone**   Current price **23⅞**

Nearby options' maturity month **August**   Striking price **25**

Long-term option maturity month **November**   Striking price **25**

Nearby option intrinsic value **0**

Nearby option time value **¹³⁄₁₆**

Nearby option premium   **¹³⁄₁₆**

Long-term option intrinsic value **0**

Long-term option time value **1⅛**

Long-term option premium   **1⅛**

B. Initial Position

(1) Sell **1** nearby options @ **¹³⁄₁₆**   for $ **81.25**

(2) Less commissions $ **N/A**

(3) Buy **1** long-term options @ **1⅛**   for $ **112.50**

(4) Plus commissions $ **N/A**

(5) Net cost $ **31.25**

C. Position Profit or Loss

The position's maximum loss will equal the net cost (5) and will occur if both the nearby and far-term options are either deep-in-the-money or deep-out-of-the-money when the near-term option expires. Under these conditions, both options will have very little time value and will be virtually equal in price.

Stock price at liquidation   **25⅛**

Days until near-term option expiration **21**

Basic Spreads 117

Nearby options' maturity month __August__ Striking price __25__

Long-term option maturity month __November__ Striking price __25__

Nearby option intrinsic value __$\frac{1}{8}$__

Nearby option time value __$\frac{3}{8}$__

Nearby option premium ____$\frac{1}{2}$____

Long-term option intrinsic value __$\frac{1}{8}$__

Long-term option time value __$1\frac{5}{8}$__

Long-term option premium ____$1\frac{3}{4}$____

(6) Buy __1__ nearby options @ __$\frac{1}{2}$__ for $ __50.00__

(7) Plus commissions $ __N/A__

(8) Sell __1__ long-term options @ __$1\frac{3}{4}$__ for $ __175.00__

(9) Plus commissions $ __N/A__

(10) Net revenues $ __125.00__

Net profit or loss [(10) − (5)] $ __93.75__

Worksheet 5-6
Time Spread Roll Forward Worksheet

A. Initial Position Data

Underlying stock __Firestone__ Current price __$23\frac{7}{8}$__

Options' striking price __25__

Nearby option''s maturity month __August__

Long-term options' maturity month __November__

Nearby option intrinsic value __0__

Nearby option time value __$\frac{13}{16}$__

Nearby option premium ____$\frac{13}{16}$____

Long-term option intrinsic value __0__

Long-term option time value __$1\frac{1}{8}$__

Long-term option premium ____$1\frac{1}{8}$____

(1) Sell **1** nearby options @ **$^{13}/_{16}$**   for $ **81.25**

(2) Less commissions $ **N/A**

(3) Buy **1** long-term options @ **$1\frac{1}{8}$**   for $ **112.50**

(4) Plus commissions $ **N/A**

(5) Net cost $ **31.25**

B. Roll-Forward Position Data

Underlying stock **Firestone**   Current price **$25\frac{1}{8}$**

Options' striking price **25**

Option premium **$\frac{1}{2}$** at maturity @ **August**

Option premium **$1\frac{3}{4}$** at maturity @ **November**

Option premium **$2\frac{1}{4}$** at maturity @ **February**

(6) Buy **1** options maturity = **August** @ **$\frac{1}{2}$** for $ **50.00**

(7) Plus commissions $ **N/A**

(8) Sell **2** options maturity = **November** @ **$1\frac{3}{4}$** for $ **350.00**

(9) Less commissions $ **N/A**

(10) Buy **1** options maturity = **February** @ **$2\frac{1}{4}$** for $ **225.00**

(11) Plus commissions $ **N/A**

(12) Roll-forward cash flow $ **75.00**

(13) Net cash flow [(12) − (5)] $ **43.75**

C. Total Position Profit or Loss

Stock price at liquidation   **25**

Days until nearby option expires **22**

Options' striking price **25**

Nearby option maturity month **November**

Long-term option maturity month **February**

Basic Spreads 119

Nearby option intrinsic value __0__

Nearby option time value __15/16__

Nearby option premium   __15/16__

Long-term option intrinsic value __0__

Long-term option time value __1¹⁵/16__

Long-term option premium   __1¹⁵/16__

(14) Buy __1__ options maturity = **November** at __15/16__ for $ __93.75__

(15) Plus Commissions $ __N/A__

(16) Sell __1__ options maturity = **February** at 1¹⁵/16 for $ __193.75__

(17) Less Commissions $ __N/A__

(18) Net Revenues $ __100.00__

Net profit or loss [(18) + (13)] $ __143.75__

The value for the roll-forward cash flow is obtained in a different manner from those of the roll-up and roll-down cash flows. In this case, the total cost of purchasing the options (line 6 plus line 10) is subtracted from the total amount of revenue generated by the sale of the options (line 8). Once again the investor is selling both options in tandem rather than separately to save commissions.

CONCLUSION

This chapter introduced three basic spreads: the bull spread, the bear spread, and the time spread. These strategies are similar in that they provide the conservative investor with relatively low-risk positions that can be profitable given any type of stock price behavior. Each of these spreads is established by combining a long position and a short position in options of the same class but of different series.

The key to success with any spread lies in establishing the long position in the option that will appreciate the most. The short position's revenue is used to reduce the cost of the long position and, hence, the spread's total cost.

120   Chapter 5

PROBLEMS

See Appendix D for solutions.

PROBLEM 5-1

Suppose that in January the 75-day Kellogg March 30 call option
has a price of 3½, the 75-day Kellogg March 35 call option has a price
of 1⅞, and the price of Kellogg's common stock is 32. Since you feel
that the price of Kellogg stock will increase during the next 75 days,
you decide to create a bull spread by purchasing the March 30 call
option and selling the March 35 call option. In March, seven days
prior to the call options' expiration, the securities are priced as follows:

Kellogg common shares, 42
Kellogg March 30 call option, 12⅛
Kellogg March 35 call option, 7⅛

Compute the bull spread's profit assuming it is liquidated seven
day prior to the March expiration date.

PROBLEM 5-2

Suppose that with 25 days until expiration, you observe that Kellogg's share price has risen to 40, the March 30 call option's price
has increased to 11, the March 35 call option is selling for 6⅛, and
the March 40 call option is selling for 2. Compute the profits generated by a roll-up from the March 30–35 bull spread to the March 35–40
bull spread assuming the spread is liquidated seven days before expiration, when the securities are valued as follows:

Kellogg common stock, 42
Kellogg March 35 call option, 7⅛
Kellogg March 40 call option, 2⅛

Basic Spreads

121

PROBLEM 5-3

Suppose that on July 1 the 135-day General Motors November 75 put option has a price of 3, the 135-day General Motors November 70 put option's price is 1⅝, and General Motors' common stock is priced at 75. Since you feel that GM's common stock price will drop during the next 135 days, you decide to create a bear spread by purchasing the November 75 put option and selling the November 70 put option. In November, four days prior to the put options' expiration, the securities are priced as follows:

GM common shares, 69
November 75 put option, 6
November 70 put option, 1⅛

Compute the bear spread's profit assuming it is liquidated four days prior to the November expiration date.

PROBLEM 5-4

Suppose that with 35 days until expiration, you observe that General Motors' share price has fallen to 70, the November 75 put option's price has increased to 6¼, the November 70 put option is selling for 2⅜, and the November 65 put option is selling for ⅞. Compute the profits generated by a roll-down from the November 70–75 bear spread to the November 65–70 bear spread assuming the spread is liquidated four days before expiration, when the securities are valued as follows:

GM common stock, 69
GM November 70 put option, 1¼
GM 65 put option, ⅛

PROBLEM 5-5

Suppose that on December 1 the 70-day Mobil Oil February 30 call option has a price of 2¾, the 165-day May call option has a price of 4, and the price of Mobil's common stock is 30. Since you feel that Mobil's common stock price will remain stable during the next two months, you decide to create a time spread by purchasing the February 30 call option and selling the May 30 call option. In February, five days prior to the February 30 call options' expiration, the securities are priced as follows:

Mobil common shares, 27
Mobil February 30 call option, ¹⁄₁₆
Mobil May 30 call option, 2⅛

Compute the time spread's profit assuming it is liquidated five days prior to the February expiration date.

PROBLEM 5-6

Suppose that with five days until the February expiration, you observe that Mobil Oil's share price has fallen to 27, the 5-day February 30 call option's price has declined to ¹⁄₁₆, the 98-day May 30 call option's price has dropped to 2⅛, and the 125-day August 30 call option is selling for 3¼. Compute the profits generated by a roll-forward from the February–May 30 time spread to the May–August 30 time spread assuming the spread is liquidated four days before the May call option's expiration, when the securities are valued as follows:

Mobil common stock, 30⅛
Mobil May 30 call option, ¼
Mobil August 30 call option, 3

Chapter
Six

COMBINATIONS

In earlier chapters, we concentrated on forming positions by using either call options or put options. In this chapter, we examine two basic strategies that rely on combining call and put options: straddles and strangles.

DEFINITIONS

A *straddle* is formed by taking similar positions in the at-the-money call options and put options of a given stock. One is *long a straddle* if one purchases an at-the-money call option and an at-the-money put option. One is *short a straddle* if one writes an at-the-money call option and an at-the-money put option.

The term *strangle* was coined by option traders and means taking similar positions in a given stock's out-of-the-money call options and out-of-the-money put options. One is *long a strangle* if one purchases out-of-the-money call options and put options. One is *short a strangle* if one sells out-of-the-money call options and put options.

UNDERLYING LOGIC

The logic behind both the straddle and the strangle consists of profiting from changes in the underlying stock's price volatility. It is wrong to assume that it is best to purchase straddles and strangles on high-volatility stocks and to write straddles and strangles on low-volatility stocks. If a stock's options are fairly valued, their market prices will accurately reflect the volatility of the stock's price.

Straddles and strangles work best when there is a great deal of uncertainty about a stock's price volatility. The logic of these strategies is based on the positive relationship of the underlying stock's price volatility to both the call and put options' premiums. In general, this positive relationship means that both call and put option prices will increase when stock price volatility rises and decrease as stock price volatility declines. This occurs because a rise in stock price volatility can result in a large increase or decrease in the underlying stock's price while a decline in volatility can lead to a very stable stock price.

If a substantial increase in a stock's price volatility is anticipated, then it is preferable to purchase a straddle. This will allow the investor to benefit from the large stock price movement via either the put option or the call option. If the increased volatility results in a large stock price increase, the call option will increase in value and the put option's value will decline. If the greater volatility causes the stock price to undergo a drastic decrease, the put option will increase in value while the call option will lose value. The maximum amount the investor can lose is the cost of the straddle: the total amount paid for both the put option and the call option.

If a significant decrease in stock price volatility is anticipated, it is better to sell a strangle than a straddle. The logic of this strategy is as follows. A decrease in stock price volatility means that the stock's price should remain stable. A stable stock price means that out-of-the-money and at-the-money options will probably be worthless at expiration, since their premiums have no intrinsic value and will decay rapidly as maturity approaches. An investor can profit from this anticipated price behavior by selling options before their premiums begin to decay. This can be accomplished by selling either a straddle or a strangle. However, in both of these cases, the seller is writing a naked call option and a naked put option. Thus, both

Exhibit 6-1
Option Prices for the Hilton October Straddle and Strangle

October Options' Maturity: T = 180 Days

Option & NY Close	Striking Price	Calls—Last			Puts—Last		
		Apr.	Jul.	Oct.	Apr.	Jul.	Oct.
Hilton	65	$5\frac{3}{16}$	$5\frac{5}{8}$	$6\frac{3}{8}$	$\frac{1}{16}$	$\frac{1}{8}$	$\frac{1}{4}$
70	70	1	$1\frac{7}{8}$	$2\frac{7}{8}$	$\frac{7}{8}$	$1\frac{3}{8}$	$1\frac{5}{8}$
70	75	$\frac{1}{8}$	$\frac{3}{8}$	$\frac{7}{8}$	$5\frac{3}{16}$	$5\frac{1}{4}$	$5\frac{3}{8}$

October Options' Maturity: T = 135 Days

Option & NY Close	Striking Price	Calls—Last			Puts—Last		
		Jul.	Oct.	Jan.	Jul.	Oct.	Jan.
Hilton	65	$5\frac{1}{4}$	6	$6\frac{3}{4}$	$\frac{1}{16}$	$\frac{1}{4}$	$\frac{7}{16}$
70	70	$1\frac{1}{4}$	$2\frac{3}{8}$	$3\frac{1}{4}$	1	$1\frac{1}{2}$	$1\frac{3}{4}$
70	75	$\frac{1}{16}$	$\frac{5}{8}$	$1\frac{3}{16}$	$5\frac{1}{8}$	$5\frac{3}{16}$	$5\frac{1}{4}$

October Options' Maturity: T = 90 Days

Option & NY Close	Striking Price	Calls—Last			Puts—Last		
		Oct.	Jan.	Apr.	Oct.	Jan.	Apr.
Hilton	65	$5\frac{5}{8}$	$6\frac{3}{8}$	7	$\frac{1}{8}$	$\frac{1}{4}$	$\frac{1}{2}$
70	70	$1\frac{7}{8}$	$2\frac{7}{8}$	$3\frac{5}{8}$	$1\frac{3}{8}$	$1\frac{5}{8}$	$1\frac{7}{8}$
70	75	$\frac{3}{8}$	$\frac{7}{8}$	$1\frac{1}{2}$	$5\frac{3}{16}$	$5\frac{3}{8}$	$5\frac{1}{2}$

October Options' Maturity: T = 45 Days

Option & NY Close	Striking Price	Calls—Last			Puts—Last		
		Oct.	Jan.	Apr.	Oct.	Jan.	Apr.
Hilton	65	$5\frac{1}{4}$	6	$6\frac{3}{4}$	$\frac{1}{16}$	$\frac{1}{4}$	$\frac{7}{16}$
70	70	$1\frac{1}{4}$	$2\frac{3}{8}$	$3\frac{1}{4}$	1	$1\frac{1}{2}$	$1\frac{3}{4}$
70	75	$\frac{1}{16}$	$\frac{5}{8}$	$1\frac{3}{16}$	$5\frac{1}{8}$	$5\frac{3}{16}$	$5\frac{1}{4}$

of these strategies are quite risky, since both have the potential for unlimited loss. Writing a straddle, however, is more risky than writing a strangle, because it will result in more rapid losses if the stock price begins to move. Since the strangle writer can withstand greater stock price movement than the straddle writer before incurring any losses, writing strangles is recommended over writing straddles.

128   Chapter 6

STRADDLE AND STRANGLE PURCHASING STRATEGIES

In this section, we will examine the strategies of purchasing straddles and strangles. In the following section, we focus on the corresponding writing strategies. Exhibit 6-1 provides data to which we will turn in our discussions of all four strategies.

STRADDLE PURCHASE   The profitability of purchasing a straddle is illustrated in Exhibits 6-1 and 6-2. In this situation, a 180-day Hilton Hotel Corporation October 70 straddle has been formed by purchasing an at-the-money Hilton call option and an at-the-money Hilton put option. Exhibit 6-1 indicates that the October at-the-money call option's premium is $2\frac{7}{8}$ and the at-the-money put option's premium is $1\frac{5}{8}$. Thus, the straddle's cost is $4\frac{1}{2}$, or $450.

In this case, Hilton's share price must move by at least the cost of the straddle, $4\frac{1}{2}$, by expiration in order for the buyer to just break even. If the price of Hilton's shares moves by more than $4\frac{1}{2}$ points to a value greater than $74\frac{1}{2}$ or less than $65\frac{1}{2}$ at the options' expiration, the straddle buyer will earn a profit. If Hilton's share price is between $65\frac{1}{2}$ and $74\frac{1}{2}$ at the options' expiration, the straddle buyer will suffer a loss. If Hilton's share price equals 70 at the options' expiration, the straddle buyer will lose the entire amount paid—$4\frac{1}{2}$ points, or $450. This is illustrated in Exhibit 6-2 by the line labeled ''T = 0.''

The remaining three lines in Exhibit 6-2 indicate the straddle's profit or loss at various points in time prior to maturity. For example, if the stock price is 70 with 135 days remaining until expiration, the position will lose $62.50 if the investor is forced to liquidate. The loss will occur because the value of the October straddle is $3\frac{7}{8}$—$2\frac{3}{8}$ for the October 70 call option and $1\frac{1}{2}$ for the October 70 put option— which is $\frac{5}{8}$ points less than the initial cost of $4\frac{1}{2}$. If the stock price remains unchanged during the straddle's life, the losses will be $1\frac{1}{4}$ points, or $125, with 90 days until expiration and $2\frac{1}{4}$ points, or $225, with 45 days until expiration.

These losses will increase as maturity approaches because of the time premium decay. Thus, it is extremely important to realize that time works against the straddle buyer in flat or unchanging markets. On the other hand, since there is no upper limit on the value of the *stock*, there is no upper limit on the profit that the straddle buyer

Combinations

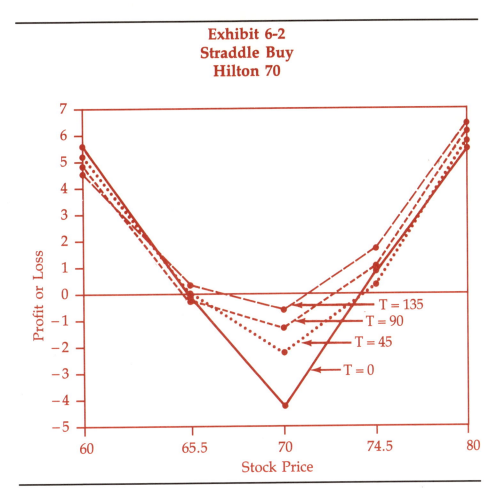

Exhibit 6-2
Straddle Buy
Hilton 70

can earn via the call option if the price of Hilton stock keeps rising. However, since the stock cannot fall below zero, the maximum profit available to the straddle buyer in a rapidly declining market through the put option is 65½ points.

STRANGLE PURCHASE Since a strangle is formed with an out-of-the-money call option and an out-of-the-money put option, it is cheaper than a straddle. Therefore, a strangle buyer has less to lose than a straddle buyer. However, the underlying stock's price must make a very large move before the strangle buyer will earn a profit—indeed, a much greater move than in the case of the straddle buyer.

Exhibit 6-1 can be used in conjunction with Exhibit 6-3 to illustrate the profit potential for a strangle buyer. Here a 180-day Hilton strangle has been constructed by purchasing the out-of-the-money October 75 call option for ⅞ and the out-of-the-money October 65 put option for ¼ for a total cost of 1⅛ points, or $125. In Exhibit 6-3, the ''T = 0'' line indicates that Hilton's share price must rise or fall by 6⅛ points in order for the strangle buyer to break even at expiration. This large price movement is necessary because either the put option or the call option must be in-the-money at expiration before the strangle buyer can break even. A 6⅛-point increase in Hilton's stock price to 76⅛ will result in the October 75 call option taking on 1⅛ points of intrinsic value. A 6⅛-point drop in the share price to 63⅞ will place the October 65 put option 1⅛ points in-the-money. If the price of Hilton common stock is between 65 and 75 at the options' expiration, both options will expire worthless, since both will be out-of-the-money. This is considerably different from the 4½-point price movement required for the straddle buyer to break even over the same time period. Thus, it is better for an investor to buy a straddle than a strangle if an increase in stock price volatility is anticipated.

In order to be consistent with our straddle purchase example, we will assume a constant stock price of 70 with 135, 90, and 45 days remaining until expiration in our discussion of the strangle's behavior. These maturities are illustrated by the three remaining lines in Exhibit 6-3.

At 135 days until expiration, the October strangle has a value of ⅞: ⅝ for the October 75 call option and ¼ for the October 65 put option. If the investor liquidates the position at this point, a ¼-point, or $25, loss will occur (1⅛ − ⅞). This is much less than the ⅝-point, or $62.50, loss that the straddle buyer would incur under the same conditions.

When there are 90 days left until expiration, the strangle's value is ½—⅜ for the October 75 call and ⅛ for the October 65 put. The strangle buyer suffers a ⅝-point (1⅛ − ½), or $62.50, loss if forced to liquidate with the Hilton share price at 70. However, this is only one-half of the 1¼-point, or $125, loss suffered by the straddle buyer in the same situation.

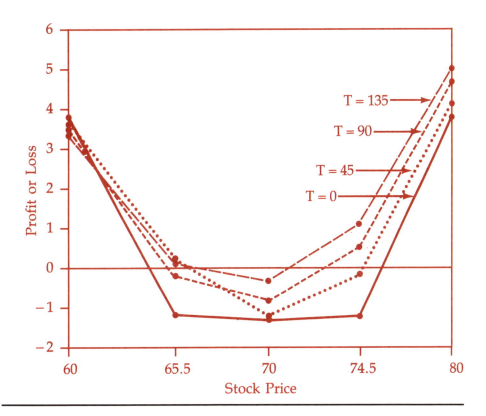

Exhibit 6-3
Strangle Buy
Hilton 75 Call, Hilton 65 Put

Finally, at 45 days to expiration the strangle's value is ⅛, since both the October 75 call option and the October 65 put option are valued at ¹⁄₁₆. Now the loss to the strangle buyer is 1 point (1⅛ − ⅛), or $100, while the straddle buyer would incur a loss of 2¼ points, or $225.

Note that time works against the strangle buyer just as it does against the straddle buyer. However, the strangle buyer loses less, because the strangle position's cost is lower than the straddle's.

STRADDLE AND STRANGLE WRITING STRATEGIES

The same October straddle and strangle used to illustrate the purchase strategies will be used to explain the writing strategies. The prices for these positions can be found in Exhibit 6-1.

STRADDLE WRITE Exhibit 6-4 portrays the profit profile for the writer of the 180-day Hilton October 70 straddle. The cash inflow to the straddle writer generated by the sale of the October 70 call option for 2⅞ points and of the October 70 put option for 1⅝ points is 4½ points, or $450.

According to the maturity line labeled ''T = 0,'' if the price of Hilton's shares is 70 at the options' maturity, both the put option and the call option will expire worthless and the straddle writer will have earned the maximum profit of 4½ points.

If the stock's price is anything other than 70 at expiration, the straddle will have some intrinsic value, which means that the straddle writer must cover the open short position. For example, if the stock's price is greater than 70 at maturity, the put option will be worthless but the call option will have intrinsic value. Thus, the straddle writer must cover the short position in the call option by purchasing a call option with an identical striking price and maturity.

If the stock price is less than 70 at expiration, the call option will be worthless and the put option will have intrinsic value. In this case, the open short position in the put option must be covered by purchasing a put option with an identical striking price and maturity.

As long as the price of the Hilton stock is between 65½ and 74½ at the straddle's maturity, the writer will earn a profit. Note that the breakeven points of 65½ and 74½ for the straddle writer are identical to those of the straddle buyer. This is logical, because the straddle writer and buyer take similar but opposite positions in the same options.

The other three maturity lines in Exhibit 6-4 show the straddle writer's profit or loss at various points in time during the straddle's life. For example, if the stock price is 70 with 135 days until expiration, the straddle writer will gain $62.50 if forced to liquidate. The gain will occur because the value of the October straddle is 3⅞ (2⅜ for the October 70 call option and 1½ for the October 70 put option),

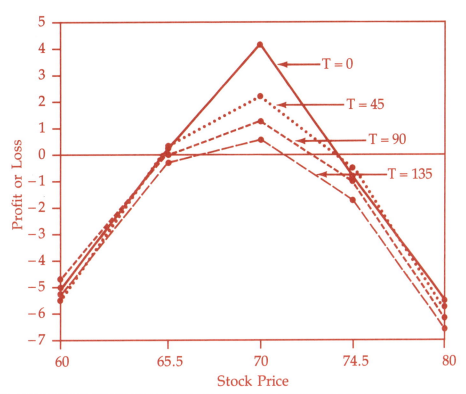

**Exhibit 6-4
Straddle Write
Hilton 70**

which is ⅝ points less than the value of the writer's initial cash inflow of 4½ points. If the stock price remains unchanged during the straddle's life, the writer's gains will be 1¼ points, or $125, with 90 days until expiration and 2¼ points, or $225, with 45 days until expiration. The straddle writer's profits rise as maturity approaches because of the time premium decay. Remember that the straddle writer has sold options that had no intrinsic value. Thus, the entire initial value of the straddle—and the writer's liability—will erode with the passage of time if the price of the underlying stock remains unchanged.

It is important to realize that in flat or unchanging markets, time works against the straddle buyer but benefits the straddle writer.

In active markets characterized by rising stock prices, the loss potential for the straddle writer is unlimited, since there is no theoretical upper limit to the liability associated with the naked call position. In falling markets, the straddle writer's maximum loss equals the put option's striking price minus the straddle's initial value and is realized if the market price of the stock falls to zero.

STRANGLE WRITE   Exhibit 6-5 can be used along with the data in Exhibit 6-1 to illustrate the strangle seller's profit potential. Here a 180- day Hilton strangle is sold by writing the out-of-the-money October 75 call option for $7/8$ and the out-of-the-money October 65 put option for $1/4$ for a total cash inflow of $1\frac{1}{8}$ points, or $125.

The "T = 0" maturity line indicates that if Hilton's share price rises or falls by $6\frac{1}{8}$ points at expiration, the strangle writer will break even. A price movement of less than $6\frac{1}{8}$ points will result in a profit for the writer, since both options will expire out-of-the-money, allowing the writer to keep the entire initial cash flow. A price movement of more than $6\frac{1}{8}$ points will cause either the put option or the call option to be in-the-money at expiration, which translates into a liability for the strangle writer that must be offset. Thus, the strangle writer will incur a loss when the liability is eliminated via the purchase of an option that has a striking price and maturity identical to those of the in-the-money option, since the purchased option will have a value greater than the initial cash inflow of $1\frac{1}{8}$ points. This is quite different from the $4\frac{1}{2}$-point price movement that the straddle writer can withstand before suffering a loss. Thus, it is preferable for an investor to write a strangle rather than a straddle if a decrease in stock price volatility is anticipated.

In the remainder of our discussion of the strangle writer's profit profile, we will again assume a constant stock price of 70 and expirations of 135, 90, and 45 days, as shown by the other three maturity lines in Exhibit 6-5.

With 135 days until expiration, the October strangle has a value of $7/8$—$5/8$ for the October 75 call option and $1/4$ for the October 65 put option. If the investor liquidates the position at this point, a $1/4$-point, or $25, gain will be realized ($1\frac{1}{8} - 7/8$). This is much less than the $5/8$-point, or $62.50, gain that the straddle buyer would enjoy under the same conditions.

Combinations

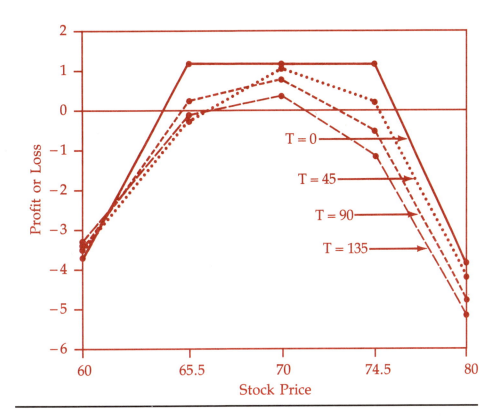

**Exhibit 6-5
Strangle Write
Hilton 75 Call, Hilton 65 Put**

When there are 90 days left until expiration, the strangle's value is ½—⅜ for the October 75 call and ⅛ for the October 65 put. Here the strangle writer earns a ⅝-point (1⅛ − ½), or $62.50, gain if forced to liquidate with the Hilton share price at 70. However, this is only one-half of the 1¼ point, or $125, profit realized by the straddle writer in the same situation.

Finally, at 45 days to expiration the strangle's value is ⅛, since both the October 75 call and the October 65 put are valued at ¹⁄₁₆. In this case, the strangle writer's gain is 1 point (1⅛ − ⅛), or $100, while the straddle writer would earn 2¼ points, or $225.

Note that time works for the strangle writer just as it does for the straddle writer. However, the strangle earns less profit, since its initial cash inflow is lower than the straddle's.

LIMITATIONS OF OPTION WRITING STRATEGIES It must be emphasized that both the straddle and strangle writing strategies will yield profits only if the investor can correctly anticipate a declining stock price volatility. If the volatility forecast is wrong and the stock price volatility does not shrink, large losses can occur. Since both of these option writing strategies have limited profit but unlimited loss potential, they are not recommended for the conservative investor. If one is determined to implement a strategy that will earn a profit in a stable market, one should use the call option time spread. Although a cash outflow is required in order to establish this spread—as opposed to a cash inflow generated by writing a straddle or a strangle—purchasing a time spread is safer and more conservative than writing either a straddle or a strangle, since the spread's maximum loss is limited. Further, its profitability compares very favorably with that of the strangle and straddle writing strategies.

ILLUSTRATIONS OF THE STRADDLE/STRANGLE POSITIONS

In this section we will examine some examples of the concepts discussed above, and use worksheets to compute the profitability of each of the four positions. These examples are based on the turmoil that surrounded Hilton Hotel Corporation in 1985, which created an ideal environment for trading straddles, strangles, and time spreads.

STRADDLE PURCHASE In January 1985, Hilton Hotel Corporation applied to the New Jersey Casino Control Commission for a license to operate its recently completed hotel and casino in Atlantic City. After taking what seemed to be an inordinate amount of time considering Hilton's request, the commission rejected the application on February 28. However, during the latter half of February, the market appeared to be anticipating approval of the application, since the price of Hilton common stock moved from 58½ to nearly 62½ and remained there until the February 28 denial. On that date, there

Combinations 137

was a dramatic increase in volume and Hilton's share price dropped by approximately 3 points. Hilton appealed the ruling, and at the end of March the New Jersey Casino Control Commission agreed to reconsider Hilton's application.

When Hilton's license application was announced on February 13, the share price of Hilton common stock was 59⅞, the May 60 call option's price was 2½, and the May 60 put option was at 2⅝. Given these conditions, an investor might have decided to purchase a May 60 straddle for 5⅛, or $512.50, in order to profit from the anticipated share price movement. A strong case can be made for the straddle purchase, since there was no guarantee that the commission would approve Hilton's license. Failure to obtain a casino license would have seriously hampered Hilton's ability to compete in Atlantic City, while issuance of it would have allowed the firm to reap the benefits of having both a hotel and a casino in that lucrative market.

Seven days later, on February 20, no decision had been announced by the commission. However, Hilton's share price had risen to 62⅞, the May 60 call option's price had increased to 4¾, and the May 60 put option's price had fallen to 1 1/16. The value of the straddle position was now 5 13/16, or $581.25.

At this point in our discussion, given the rapid increase in Hilton's stock price and the resulting rise in the call option's price, it is appropriate to introduce the concept of ''legging out'' of the long straddle position. In general, the term *legging out* refers to closing out one side of a spread or combination in an attempt to maximize the net gains associated with an anticipated security price movement. It is important to understand that legging out of a combination means assuming a relatively higher level of risk, since the new position is an open position in the remaining option. The conservative investor should be extremely cautious about legging out of a combination based on an anticipated stock price movement. Recall that the basic logic of the combination—whether straddle or strangle—consists of attempting to profit from a change in the underlying stock's price volatility. One is not seeking to predict the direction of the security's price movement. Thus, the combination's purpose is defeated if one legs out prematurely.

In this example, the straddle buyer might have been tempted to leg out of the long straddle position on February 20, because approval of Hilton's license request was anticipated and likely to result in further increases in the prices of both Hilton's common shares and call options. If the straddle buyer legged out of the position by selling the May 60 put option for $1\frac{1}{16}$, the resulting value of the long May 60 call position would have been $4\frac{3}{4}$, with a net cost of $4\frac{1}{16}$—$5\frac{1}{8}$ paid for the straddle less the $1\frac{1}{16}$ received for selling the put option.

On March 1, the New Jersey Casino Control Commission announced that it had rejected Hilton's license application. Hilton's common stock fell to $57\frac{5}{8}$, the May 60 call option closed at $2\frac{1}{4}$, the May 60 put option closed at $3\frac{3}{8}$, and the value of the May 60 straddle ended the day at $5\frac{5}{8}$, or \$562.50. At this point, it seems reasonable to conclude that the market had adjusted the prices of Hilton's shares and options to reflect the commission's decision. Thus, it seemed unlikely that the security prices would experience any further significant changes in the near future. Therefore, the straddle buyer should have closed out the position and taken the $\frac{1}{2}$ point, or \$50, profit. The straddle buyer who decided to leg out of the long straddle position by selling the May 60 put option would not have fared as well— indeed, the decline in the stock's price and the accompanying drop in the May 60 call option's price would have resulted in a $1\frac{13}{16}$-point, or \$181.25, loss for this investor. This example clearly illustrates the risk inherent in legging out of a combination.

Worksheet 6-1 illustrates the potential gains and losses for the Hilton May 60 straddle purchase. The first section, "Position Data," summarizes the relevant information for the straddle buyer. The second section, "Initial Position," computes the straddle's exact cost. The final section, "Position Profit or Loss," calculates the straddle's profit or loss. It is completed at liquidation or expiration of the position, whichever occurs first. In this example, the straddle buyer did not wait for expiration but decided to liquidate the position after 16 days.

STRADDLE SALE During the first two weeks of March following the license denial, the price of Hilton's common shares remained fairly stable and closed at 58 on March 15. However, over the following two weeks the share price rose dramatically to a closing value of $72\frac{1}{4}$ on April 3. This substantial increase was caused by

Combinations

139

Worksheet 6-1
Straddle Purchase Worksheet

A. Position Data

Underlying stock __Hilton__   Current price __59⅞__

Days until option expiration __92__

Call option maturity month __May__   Striking price __60__

Put option maturity month __May__   Striking price __60__

Call option intrinsic value __0__

Call option time value __2½__

Call option premium   __2½__

Put option intrinsic value __⅛__

Put option time value __2½__

Put option premium   __2⅝__

B. Initial Position

(1) Buy __1__ calls @ __2½__   for $ __250.00__

(2) Plus commissions $ __N/A__

(3) Buy __1__ put @ __2⅝__   for $ __262.50__

(4) Plus commissions $ __N/A__

(5) Net cost $ __512.50__

C. Position Profit or Loss

The position's maximum loss will equal the net cost (5) and will occur if the stock price equals the options' exercise price at maturity. Under these conditions, both options will expire worthless.

Stock price at liquidation   __57⅝__

Days until option expiration __76__

Call option intrinsic value __0__

Call option time value __2¼__

Call option premium	2¼
Put option intrinsic value 2⅜	
Put option time value 1	
Put option premium	3⅜
Straddle value	$ 562.50
(6) Sell 1 calls @ 2¼	for	$ 225.00
(7) Less commissions	$ N/A
(8) Sell 1 puts @ 3⅜	for	$ 337.50
(9) Less commissions	$ N/A
(10) Net revenues	$ 562.50
Net profit or loss [(10) − (5)]	$ 50.00

Golden Nugget Corporation's offer of $72 a share for Hilton common stock on that day. The offer was good for 10 days—until April 12—but was deemed inadequate by Hilton's chairman when it was made public on April 4. Given this set of circumstances, it seems that a straddle sale would have been the appropriate strategy, since the share price would not have fluctuated significantly during the offer's life.

On April 4, the closing price of Hilton's common shares was 69⅝ and both the May 70 call and put options closed at 3⅞. Thus, a straddle writer would have been able to take in 7¾ points, or $775, from the sale of the put and call.

During the offer's life, Hilton took action to ward off the takeover, which Golden Nugget attempted to counter. This resulted in the share price rising to a high of 71⅞, the call option increasing to 5, and the put option falling to 3 on April 8, for a straddle value of 8. However, this price rise was short-lived: On April 12, the offer's expiration date, the share price had fallen to 68, the call had dropped to 2⅝, and the put had risen to 4⅜, resulting in a straddle value of 7, or $700. Because Golden Nugget's offer expired without being accepted, it was very likely that the share price would differ dramatically from the offer's value of $72 in the near future. Thus, the straddle seller should have liquidated. Worksheet 6-2 illustrates the computation of the straddle seller's gain.

Combinations 141

Worksheet 6-2
Straddle Sale Worksheet

A. Position Data

Underlying stock __Hilton__   Current price __$69\frac{5}{8}$__

Days until option expiration __42__

Call options' maturity month __May__   Striking price __70__

Put option maturity month __May__   Striking price __70__

Call option intrinsic value __0__

Call option time value __$3\frac{7}{8}$__

Call option premium __$3\frac{7}{8}$__

Put option intrinsic value __$\frac{3}{8}$__

Put option time value __$3\frac{1}{2}$__

Put option premium __$3\frac{7}{8}$__

B. Initial position

(1) Sell __1__ calls @ __$3\frac{7}{8}$__   for $ __387.50__

(2) Less commissions $ __N/A__

(3) Sell __1__ puts @ __$3\frac{7}{8}$__   for $ __387.50__

(4) Less commissions $ __N/A__

(5) Net revenues $ __775.00__

C. Position Profit or Loss

The position's maximum loss has no upper limit. Large losses will occur if the stock's price is much greater than the call option's exercise price or less than the put option's exercise price at maturity.

Stock price at liquidation __68__

Days until option expiration __33__

Call option intrinsic value __0__

Call option time value __$2\frac{5}{8}$__

Call option premium		2⅝
Put option intrinsic value __2__		
Put option time value __2⅜__		
Put option premium		4⅜
Straddle value		700.00
(6) Buy __1__ calls @ __2⅝__	for $	262.50
(7) Plus commissions	$	N/A
(8) Buy __1__ puts @ __4⅜__	for $	437.50
(9) Plus commissions	$	N/A
(10) Net costs		700.00
Net profit or loss [(5) − (10)]	$	75.00

In the above examples, the various security price changes illustrate the straddle's behavior in a volatile market. However, it must be emphasized that if there had been commission charges, then the ½-point profit probably would have been too small to cover the straddle buyer's round-trip costs. The same is true for the straddle seller: A ¾-point profit probably would have been too small to offset the round-trip commission charges. Thus, it seems that the fundamental criterion for constructing a straddle—that is, having a better estimate than the market of the stock price's volatility—would not have been met in either situation.

These examples were chosen to show the conservative investor how difficult it is to outguess the market and how closely these positions must be monitored. Moreover, it is imperative that the investor be aware of the total profit-and-loss potential of any position prior to investing.

STRANGLE SALE AND PURCHASE On April 15, three days after its offer expired, Golden Nugget said that it was willing to negotiate the terms of its $72-a-share offer. This was unacceptable to Hilton's board of directors, and they accelerated their efforts to get the shareholders to approve antitakeover measures at the annual meeting scheduled for May 6. Given that the issue would be decided

Combinations

within the next three weeks and that the actions of the opposing forces probably would keep Hilton's shares within a narrow trading range, selling a strangle probably would have been a good strategy in this situation. Thus, on April 15, with Hilton common stock trading at 67⅝, a May strangle could have been sold for 4¼ points, or $425, since the May 65 put option was selling for 1¾ and the May 70 call option for 2½.

During the following two weeks, Golden Nugget attacked Hilton's management on two fronts. First, on April 22 it filed a lawsuit to prevent Hilton's management from voting a block of shares, equal to 27.4 percent of the outstanding shares, in favor of the antitakeover measures. On that day, Hilton common stock closed at 66⅜, the May 65 put settled at 1⅜, and the May 70 call closed at 1¼, which translates into a strangle value of 2⅝, or $262.50. Second, on May 2 Golden Nugget launched a proxy fight designed to block the approval of the antitakeover measures at the May 6 shareholders' meeting. At the end of the day's trading activity, the stock's value was 66¾, the May 65 put option's value was ¹¹⁄₁₆, and the May 70 call option's value was 1⅞; hence, the strangle's value would have been 2⁹⁄₁₆, or $256.25.

At the May 6 shareholders' meeting, an overwhelming majority of stockholders approved the antitakeover measures, which effectively eliminated the Golden Nugget takeover threat. Since the circumstances that had precipitated the sale of the strangle were no longer in effect, it would have been time to close out the position. At liquidation, the stock price was 63¾, the May 65 put option was at 2, and the May 70 call option was at ⁵⁄₁₆. Given these prices, the strangle writer would have liquidated the position at 2⁵⁄₁₆, or $231.25, for a profit of $193.75 ($425 − $231.25).

Worksheet 6-3 provides the profit-and-loss computations for the strangle seller. Worksheet 6-4 illustrates the corresponding computations for the strangle buyer.

144   Chapter 6

Worksheet 6-3
Strangle Sale Worksheet

A. Position Data

Underlying stock __Hilton__ Current price __$67\frac{5}{8}$__

Days until option expiration __31__

Call option maturity month __May__ Striking price __70__

Put option maturity month __May__ Striking price __65__

Call option intrinsic value __0__

Call option time value __$2\frac{1}{2}$__

Call option premium   __$2\frac{1}{2}$__

Put option intrinsic value __0__

Put option time value __$1\frac{3}{4}$__

Put option premium   __$1\frac{3}{4}$__

B. Initial Position

(1) Sell __1__ calls @ __$2\frac{1}{2}$__   for $ __250.00__

(2) Less commissions $ __N/A__

(3) Sell __1__ put @ __$1\frac{3}{4}$__   for $ __175.00__

(4) Less commissions $ __N/A__

(5) Net revenues $ __425.00__

C. Position Profit or Loss

The position's maximum loss has no upper limit. Large losses will
occur if the stock's price is much greater than the call option's
exercise price or much less than the put option's exercise price
at maturity.

Stock price at liquidation   __$63\frac{3}{4}$__

Days until option expiration __10__

Call option intrinsic value __0__

Call option time value __$\frac{5}{16}$__

Combinations

Call option premium ⟶ $\frac{5}{16}$

Put option intrinsic value __0__

Put option time value __2__

Put option premium ⟶ __2__

Straddle value ⟶ $ __231.25__

(6) Buy __1__ calls @ __$\frac{5}{16}$__   for $ __31.25__

(7) Plus commissions ⟶ $ __N/A__

(8) Buy __1__ puts @ __2__   for $ __200.00__

(9) Plus commissions ⟶ $ __N/A__

(10) Net costs ⟶ $ __231.25__

Net profit or loss [(5) – (10)] ⟶ $ __193.75__

Worksheet 6-4
Strangle Puchase Worksheet

A. Position Data

Underlying stock __Hilton__   Current price __$67\frac{5}{8}$__

Days until option expiration __31__

Call options' maturity month __May__   Striking price __70__

Put option maturity month __May__   Striking price __65__

Call option intrinsic value __0__

Call option time value __$2\frac{1}{2}$__

Call option premium ⟶ __$2\frac{1}{2}$__

Put option intrinsic value __0__

Put option time value __$1\frac{3}{4}$__

Put option premium ⟶ __$1\frac{3}{4}$__

B. Initial position

(1) Buy __1__ calls @ __$2\frac{1}{2}$__   for $ __250.00__

(2) Plus commissions ⟶ $ __N/A__

(3) Buy _____1_____ puts @ _____1¾_____   for $ __175.00__

(4) Plus commissions $ ___N/A___

(5) Net cost $ __425.00__

C. Position Profit or Loss

The position's maximum loss will equal the net cost (5) and will occur if the stock price is between the options exercise price at maturity. Under these conditions, both options will expire worthless.

Stock price at liquidation $63¾$

Days until option expiration ___10___

Call option intrinsic value ___0___

Call option time value ___$\frac{5}{16}$___

Call option premium $\frac{5}{16}$

Put option intrinsic value ___0___

Put option time value ___2___

Put option premium   2

Straddle value   231.25

(6) Sell _____1_____ calls @ ___$\frac{5}{16}$___   for $ __31.25__

(7) Less commissions $ ___N/A___

(8) Sell _____1_____ puts @ _____2_____   for $ __200.00__

(9) Less commissions $ ___N/A___

(10) Net revenues   231.24

Net profit or loss [(10) − (5)] $ __193.75__

TIME SPREAD PURCHASE   Earlier we mentioned that purchasing a time spread is recommended over the sale of either a straddle or a strangle if one is attempting to profit from a flat, or stable, market in the underlying stock. Worksheet 6-5 contains the calculations for an investor who purchased a May–November 65 call option time spread on April 15 and closed out the position on May 6. Note that

Combinations   147

the 1¼-point profit is considerably smaller than the $1^{15}/_{16}$-point profit earned by the strangle writer. However, the maximum possible loss of $2^5/_8$ for the spread buyer is much less than the strangle writer's unlimited loss.

Worksheet 6-5
Time Spread Purchase Worksheet

A. Position Data

Underlying stock __Hilton__ Current price __$67^5/_8$__

Days until near-term option expiration __31__

Nearby options' maturity month __May__ Striking price __70__

Long-term option maturity month __November__ Striking price __70__

Nearby option intrinsic value __0__

Nearby option time value __$2^1/_2$__

Nearby option premium   __$2^1/_2$__

Long-term option intrinsic value __0__

Long-term option time value __$5^1/_8$__

Long-term option premium   __$5^1/_8$__

B. Initial Position

(1) Sell __1__ nearby options @ __$2^1/_2$__   for $ __250.00__

(2) Less commissions $ __N/A__

(3) Buy __1__ long-term options @ __$5^1/_8$__   for $ __512.50__

(4) Plus commissions $ __N/A__

(5) Net cost $ __262.50__

C. Position Profit or Loss

The position's maximum loss will equal the net cost (5) and will occur if both the nearby and far-term options are either deep-in-the-money or deep-out-of-the-money when the near-term option expires. Under these conditions, both options will have very little time value and will be virtually equal in price.

Stock price at liquidation		63¾
Days until near-term option expiration	10	
Nearby options' maturity month **May** Striking price	70	
Long-term option maturity month **November** Striking price	70	
Nearby option intrinsic value	0	
Nearby option time value	1⅛	
Nearby option premium		1⅛
Long-term option intrinsic value	0	
Long-term option time value	5	
Long-term option premium		5
(6) Buy __1__ nearby options @ __1⅛__	for	$ 112.50
(7) Plus commissions		$ N/A
(8) Sell __1__ long-term options @ __5__	for	$ 500.00
(9) Plus commissions		$ N/A
(10) Net revenues		$ 387.50
Net profit or loss [(10) − (5)]		$ 125.00

CONCLUSION

This chapter introduced two basic strategies known as straddles and strangles. The first part of the chapter explained the positions' underlying logic and provided a graphical analysis of their behavior overtime. The remainder of the chapter was devoted to examining the profits and losses of various positions in terms of the turmoil that surrounded Hilton Hotel Corporation in 1985. Worksheets were provided to facilitate the explanation of each trading strategy.

Both the straddle and strangle strategies combine call options and put options, are subject to unlimited gains as well as unlimited losses, and are predicated upon estimating the underlying stock's volatility more accurately than the market as a whole. The basic difference between the strategies is that the straddle uses at-the-money options while the strangle employs out-of-the-money options. Given this

Combinations   149

fundamental difference, straddles are much more sensitive to changes in the underlying stock's price than are strangles.

PROBLEMS

See Appendix D for solutions.

PROBLEM 6-1

Suppose that in early May, GTE Corporation's common stock is trading at 34⅛. You believe that a large price movement is imminent, but you do not know whether it will take the form of an increase or a decrease. Therefore, you decide to buy a GTE straddle. At this time, the 125-day September GTE 35 call option is selling for 3½ and the 125-day September GTE 35 put option is selling for 3⅜. In mid-August, approximately four weeks prior to the options' expiration, GTE common stock is trading at 40⅛, the September 35 call is at 7¼, and the closing price for the September 35 put is 1. Compute the profits generated by your straddle purchase.

PROBLEM 6-2

Use the information on GTE Corporation presented in Problem 6-1 to compute the losses that a straddle writer would incur.

PROBLEM 6-3

Suppose that in early January, Digital Equipment Corporation's common stock is trading at 104⅛. You believe that the stock price will remain relatively stable as it has for the past quarter, but you want to protect yourself as much as possible from Digital's notoriously erratic price changes. Thus, you decide to sell a Digital strangle. At

150 Chapter 6

this time, the 108-day April Digital 110 call option is selling for 8¼ and the 108-day April Digital 100 put option is selling for 6¾. In mid-March, approximately four weeks before the April options' expiration, Digital common stock is trading at 172⅞, the April 110 call option is at 63, and the closing price for the April 100 put option is 1/16. Compute the losses resulting from the sale of your strangle.

PROBLEM 6-4

Use the information on Digital Equipment Corporation given in Problem 6-3 to compute the profits that a strangle purchaser would enjoy.

Chapter Seven

ADVANCED OPTION STRATEGIES

In this chapter, we will use a different approach than in previous chapters. Here we will utilize more than one strategy at the same time, building on the basic strategies covered in Chapters One through Six. We recommend that you have a thorough grasp of the fundamental strategies before proceeding with this chapter.

The first three strategies are all bullish in nature, but each entails a unique perspective.

BUYING STOCK AND SELLING PUTS SIMULTANEOUSLY

DEFINITION AND LOGIC The strategy of *buying stock and simultaneously selling puts* is feasible when the investor is fundamentally bullish on a company but wants to purchase only a percentage of the desired position. In other words, the investor wants to dollar cost average the position. After buying a percentage of the position, the investor incurs the obligation to average down, that is, purchase more stock at a lower price.

To utilize this strategy, the investor purchases at least 100 shares of stock and simultaneously sells a put option on that stock with

154   Chapter 7

a striking price at or below the current stock price. By selling a put option, the investor makes an obligation to purchase the stock at the striking price until the option's expiration date. In return for this obligation, the investor receives a premium. If the stock is at or above the striking price at expiration, the option will expire worthless and the investor will have earned the premium as profit and at the same time realized a gain from the long stock position. If the stock is below the striking price at expiration, the option will most likely be exercised and the investor will have to purchase the stock at the striking price. However, the cost basis on the stock that is put to the investor will be the striking price less the premium received.

ILLUSTRATION: HERSHEY FOODS CORPORATION To better understand this strategy, let us take a look at a realistic situation. Suppose you like the long-term prospects for Hershey Foods Corporation. The company has a history of consistent sales and earnings growth. The stock looks attractive, but you are not sure that you want to purchase a full position on it at its current price level. You observe that Hershey common stock is trading at $27 a share and the put options are priced as follows:

Hershey 6-month 25 put, 1½
Hershey 6-month 30 put, 4½

If your intention is to own 400 shares of Hershey Foods, you execute the following strategy: Purchase 200 shares of Hershey for $27 a share, and simultaneously sell two 6-month out-of-the-money puts with a striking price of 25 for 1½ points each. Thus, your cost basis on these first 200 shares is 25½ per share:

27 (stock price per share) – 1½ (put option premium)

If the stock is at or above 25 at expiration, the put will expire worthless and your profit will be any amount above 25½. If Hershey common stock declines to below 25 at expiration, you will have to fulfill your obligation and purchase 200 shares at $25 each. Thus, your cost basis on all 400 shares will be 25¼:

27 (original stock price) – 1½ (option premium) + 25 (put striking price)

Advanced Option Strategies

155

This strategy is intended to run throughout the option's life. However, remember that you may cancel your obligation at any time by purchasing a put option in the options market with the same striking price and expiration date. In this scenario, your cost basis would be 25¼, which is 1¾ points below what you were originally willing to pay for Hershey common stock.

Note that all collateral requirements for the naked puts are probably fulfilled by the long stock position. We recommend that you consult your broker for the most current option margin requirements.

Worksheet 7-1 illustrates the computations involved in this strategy. Worksheet 7-2 fills in the data for our Hershey Foods example.

Worksheet 7-1
Buying Stock and Selling Puts Simultaneously

Common stock _____   Current price _____

Put option _____ _____ _____
           month   striking   premium
                     price

Days until expiration _____

A. Initial Position

(1) Buy _____ of _____ @ _____   = $ _____
        no. of   common   price
        shares   stock

(2) Plus commissions   + _____

(3) Net stock position $ _____

(4) Sell _____ puts @ _____ $ _____
        no.   premium

(5) Less commissions   − _____

(6) Net put options proceeds   = $ _____

(7) Net cost of positon [(3) − (6)] $ _____

(8) Net cost per share [(7)/(no. of shares purchased)] $ _____

156   Chapter 7

B.   Result of Position If Put Are Exercised
(Occurs if stock is below striking price)

(9) Buy _____ of _____ @ _____   = $ _____
      no. of   stock   put striking
      shares   price

(10) Plus commissions   + _____

(11) Cost of shares put to you   = $ _____

(12) Cost of original shares purchased (7)   + _____

(13) Net cost of total shares   = $ _____

(14) Net cost per share [(13)/(no. of shares)] $ _____

If stock is at or above striking price, your cost basis is (8).

Worksheet 7-2
Buying Stock and Selling Puts Simultaneously:
Hershey Foods Corporation

Common stock **Hershey Foods**   Current price ___**27**___

Put option _**June**_ __**25**__ _**1½**_
         month   striking premium
                 price

Days until expiration __**182**__

A.   Initial Position

(1) Buy __**200**__ of **Hershey** @ __**27**__   = $ __**5,400**__
     no. of   common   price
     shares   stock

(2) Plus commission   + __**N/A**__

(3) Net stock position $ __**5,400**__

(4) Sell __**2**__ puts @ __**1½**__ $ __**300**__
     no.   premium

(5) Less commissions   – __**N/A**__

(6) Net put options proceeds   = $ __**300**__

Advanced Option Strategies

(7) Net cost of positon [(3) – (6)] $ **5,100**

(8) Net cost per share [(7)/(no. of shares purchased)] $ **25½**

B.   Result of Position If Put Are Exercised
      (Occurs if stock is below striking price)

(9) Buy __**200**__ of __**Hershey**__ @ __**25**__   = $ **5,000**
       no. of   stock   put striking
       shares   price

(10) Plus commissions   + **N/A**

(11) Cost of shares put to you   = $ **5,000**

(12) Cost of original shares purchased (7)   + **5,100**

(13) Net cost of total shares   = $ **10,100**

(14) Net cost per share [(13)/(no. of shares)] $ **25¼**

If stock is at or above striking price, your cost basis is (8).

COVERED COMBINATIONS

Our next strategy—selling covered combinations—is also bullish. It builds on the strategy of buying stock and simultaneously selling puts.

DEFINITION AND LOGIC   Selling a covered combination is more conservative than our previous strategy of buying stock and selling puts simultaneously, because the investor receives more option premium and contracts to sell the stock at a predetermined price. In fact, a covered combination strategy is similar to covered call writing but somewhat more aggressive, because it obligates the investor to purchase more stock at a lower price.

In simplified terms, a *covered combination* is a covered call write with the simultaneous sale of puts. An investor utilizes this strategy when he or she is bullish on a particular stock but is willing to lock in a profit at a specific price and incur an obligation to average down in price. Technically, a covered combination involves the purchase of a common stock, the sale of a put with a striking price at or below

158   Chapter 7

the current stock price, and the sale of a call with a striking price
or act above the current stock price. The maximum profit potential
is the premiums received from the sale of the options plus the call
striking price minus the initial stock price. On the downside, the
investor is protected by the amount of premiums received for the
sale of the put and call.

ILLUSTRATION: HERSHEY FOODS CORPORATION To better understand the mechanics and philosophy of this strategy, let
us examine a real-life situation, again using Hershey Foods Corporation. You observe that Hershey common stock is trading at $27
a share and the options are priced as follows:

Hershey 6-month 25 put, 1½
Hershey 6-month 30 put, 4½
Hershey 6-month 25 call, 4
Hershey 6-month 30 call, 2

If your intentions are to own 400 shares of Hershey Foods, you execute the following strategy: Purchase 200 shares of Hershey for $27
a share, and simultaneously sell two 6-month out-of-the-money puts
with a striking price of 25 for 1½ points and two out-of-the-money
calls with a striking price of 30 for 2 points. Thus, your cost basis
for this position will be 23.5:

$$27 \text{ (stock price per share)} - 1\frac{1}{2} \text{ (put option premium)} -$$
$$2 \text{ (call option premium)}$$

You have made an obligation to purchase 200 more shares if the
stock is below $25 at expiration and to relinquish, or sell, the long
position of 200 shares of Hershey at $30 a share if the stock is at
or above 30. If called away at $30 a share, you will realize a gain
of 6½ points, or 27.6 percent unannualized:

$$\frac{30 \text{ (striking price)} - 23\frac{1}{2} \text{ (cost basis)}}{23\frac{1}{2} \text{ (cost basis)}}$$

In addition, your return will be enhanced by the $54 received in
dividends.

This strategy is potentially more appealing than a covered call
write, because you contract to sell stock at the same price yet increase

Advanced Option Strategies   159

your return since you receive the premium from the sale of the out-of-the-money puts, which obligates you to purchase more stock at a lower price.

Worksheet 7-3 illustrates the computations for use in the covered combination strategy. Worksheet 7-4 fills in the data from our Hershey Foods example.

Worksheet 7-3
Selling Covered Combinations

Common stock _____ Current price _____

Put option _____ _____ _____
         month   striking   premium
                price

Call option _____ _____ _____
         month   striking   premium
                price

Days until expiration _____

A. Initial Position

(1) Buy _____ of _____ @ _____   = $ _____
      no. of   common   price
      shares   stock

(2) Plus commissions   + _____

(3) Net stock position $ _____

(4) Sell _____ calls @ _____ $ _____
      no.   premium

(5) Less commissions   − _____

(6) Net call option proceeds   = $ _____

(7) Sell _____ puts @ _____ $ _____
      no.   premium

(8) Less commissions   − _____

(9) Net put options proceeds   = $ _____

(10) Net investment [(3) − (6) − (9)] $ _____

B. Maximum Profit

Increase in Stock Price

If stock is above call option striking price at expiration, call options will be exercised.

(11) Sell _____ shares of _____ @ _____ = $ _____
       amount   common   call
       in (1)   stock   striking
                              price

(12) Less commissions   − _____

(13) Plus dividends received   + _____

(14) Net proceeds $ _____

(15) Profit [(14) − (10)] $ _____

(16) Return on investment [(15)/(10)]   _____ %

(17) Return annualized [(365)/(days until expiration) × (16)]   _____ %

Decrease in Stock Price

If stock is below put option striking price at expiration, put options will be exercised.

(18) Buy _____ shares of _____ @ _____ = $ _____
       amount   common   put
       in (1)   stock   strking
                              price

(19) Plus commission   + _____

(20) Net cost of new shares   = $ _____

(21) Average cost of all shares per share
[(10) + (20) − (amount of dividends received)/
(total no. of shares)] $ _____

Neutral

If stock is between put and call striking prices at expiration, neither option will be exercised.

(22) Profit [(current value of shares) + (13) − (10)] $ _____

(23) Return on investment [(22)/(10)]   _____ %

(24) Return annualized [(365)/(days until expiration) × (23)]   _____ %

Advanced Option Strategies

161

Worksheet 7-4
Selling Covered Combinations:
Hershey Foods Corporation

Common stock ___**Hershey Foods**___ Current price ___**27**___

Put option ___**June**___ ___**25**___ ___**1½**___
month   striking   premium
         price

Call option ___**June**___ ___**30**___ ___**2**___
month   striking   premium
         price

Days until expiration ___**182**___

A. Initial Position

(1) Buy ___**200**___ of ___**Hershey**___ @ ___**27**___   = $ ___**5,400**___
     no. of   common   price
     shares   stock

(2) Plus commissions   + ___**N/A**___

(3) Net stock position $ ___**5,400**___

(4) Sell ___**2**___ calls @ ___**2**___ $ ___**400**___
      no.   premium

(5) Less commissions   − ___**N/A**___

(6) Net call option proceeds   = $ ___**400**___

(7) Sell ___**2**___ puts @ ___**1½**___ $ ___**300**___
      no.   premium

(8) Less commissions   − ___**N/A**___

(9) Net put options proceeds   = $ ___**300**___

(10) Net investment [(3) − (6) − (9)] $ ___**4,700**___

162   Chapter 7

B.   Maximum Profit

Increase in Stock Price

If stock is above call option striking price at expiration, call options
will be exercised.

(11) Sell __200__ shares of __Hershey__ @ __30__ = $ __6,000__
      amount   common   call
      in (1)   stock   strking
                                           price

(12) Less commissions   – __N/A__

(13) Plus dividends received   + __54__

(14) Net proceeds $ __6,054__

(15) Profit [(14) – (10)] $ __1,354__

(16) Return on investment [(15)/(10)]   __28.8__ %

(17) Return annualized [(365)/(days until
          expiration) × (16)]   __57.76__ %

Decrease in Stock Price

If stock is below put option striking price at expiration, put options
will be exercised.

(18) Buy __200__ shares of __Hershey__ @ __25__ = $ __5,000__
      amount   common   put
      in (1)   stock   strking
                                           price

(19) Plus commission   + __N/A__

(20) Net cost of new shares   = $ __5,000__

(21) Average cost of all shares per share
          [(10) + (20) – (amount of dividends received)/
          (total no. of shares)] $ __24.12__

Neutral

If stock is between put and call striking prices at expiration, neither
option will be exercised.

(22) Profit [(current value of shares) + (13) – (10)] $ __754__

(23) Return on investment [(22)/(10)]   __16__ %

(24) Return annualized [(365)/(days until
          expiration) × (23)]   __32__ %

*For example purposes, assume Hershey is at 27 at expiration.

Advanced Option Strategies   163

HEDGED COVERED CALL WRITE

In this section, we demonstrate a bullish yet defensive strategy that is advantageous in an increasingly volatile stock market—the hedged covered call write.

DEFINITION AND LOGIC   A *hedged covered call* gives the investor upside potential as well as protection against a severe decline in the stock's price. The basic strategy involves purchasing a minimum of 100 shares of stock, selling an out-of-the-money call, and using the proceeds from the sale to pay for a put that will act as an additional shield.

ILLUSTRATION: BOEING CORPORATION   In order to fully appreciate the hedged covered call strategy, let's take a look at a realistic situation. Suppose you are bullish on Boeing Corporation. It appears that Boeing has earnings momentum, but the common stock has already increased substantially. Boeing common stock is trading at $52 a share, and the options are priced as follows:

Boeing 6-month 50 put, 2½
Boeing 6-month 55 put, 5½
Boeing 6-month 50 call, 6½
Boeing 6-month 55 call, 3½

To use the hedged covered call strategy, you purchase 200 shares of Boeing for $52 a share, buy two 6-month 50 puts, and sell two 6-month 55 calls. Your cost basis is 51:

52 (stock price) − 3½ (call premium) + 2½ (put premium)

This is actually 1 point below the current market price.

Recall that the put gives you the right to sell Boeing at $50 a share and thus limit your risk to $1 a share. At the same time, you are making an obligation to sell Boeing for $55 a share. If called away, you will have a profit of 4 points [55 (call option striking price) − 51 (cost basis) + dividends]. This strategy is essentially a covered call write in which you are using the call option premium to pay for the put option or insurance.

164   Chapter 7

Worksheet 7-5 presents the computations for the hedged covered call write. Worksheet 7-6 completes our example with data for Boeing Corporation.

Worksheet 7-5
Hedged Covered Call Write

Common stock _____   Current price _____

Put option _____   _____   _____
              month   striking   premium
                          price

Call option _____   _____   _____
               month   striking   premium
                          price

Days until expiration _____

A. Initial Position

(1) Buy _____ of _____ @ _____   = $ _____
          no. of   common   price
          shares   stock

(2) Plus commissions   + _____

(3) Net stock investment $ _____

(4) Sell _____ calls at _____ $ _____
            no.   premium

(5) Less commissions   − _____

(6) Net call option proceeds $ _____

(7) Buy _____ puts at _____ $ _____
           no.   premium

(8) Plus commissions   + _____

(9) Net put option investment   = $ _____

(10) Net investment [(3) − (6) + (9)] $ _____

Advanced Option Strategies

B. Maximum Profit

Increase in Stock Price

If stock is above call option striking price at expiration, call options will be exercised.

(11) Sell _____ shares of _____ @ _____ = $ _____
          amount   common   call
          in (1)   stock   strking
                                    price

(12) Less commissions   – _____

(13) Plus dividends received   + _____

(14) Net proceeds   = $ _____

(15) Profit [(14) – (10)] $ _____

(16) Return on investment [(15)/(10)]   _____ %

(17) Return annualized [(365)/(days until expiration) × (16)]   _____ %

C. Maximum Risk

If stock falls below put option striking price, put options will be exercised.

(18) Sell _____ shares of _____ @ _____ = $ _____
          amount   common   put
          in (1)   stock   strking
                                      price

(19) Less commissions   – _____

(20) Plus dividends received   + $ _____

(21) Net proceeds   = $ _____

(22) Potential loss [(10) – (21)] $ _____

(23) Percentage risk [(22)/(10)]   _____ %

*You may choose to sell the put options for a profit and continue to hold the stock if you remain bullish.

D. Breakeven at Expiration

If stock is below call striking price and above put striking price, both options will expire worthless, and the average cost per share is:

(24) [(10) – (13) + (commissions to sell stock)/
     (no. of shares)]   _____

166

Chapter 7

Worksheet 7-6
Hedged Covered Call Write:
Boeing Corporation

Common stock **Boeing** Current price **52**

Put option **June** **50** **2½**
month striking premium
price

Call option **June** **55** **3½**
month striking premium
price

Days until expiration **182**

A. Initial Position

(1) Buy **200** of **Boeing** @ **52** = $ **10,400**
no. of common price
shares stock

(2) Plus commissions + **N/A**

(3) Net stock position $ **10,400**

(4) Sell **2** calls @ **3½** $ **700**
no. premium

(5) Less commissions − **N/A**

(6) Net call option proceeds $ **700**

(7) Buy **2** puts at **2½** $ **500**
no. premium

(8) Plus commissions + **N/A**

(9) Net put option investment = $ **500**

(10) Net investment [(3) − (6) + (9)] $ **10,200**

Advanced Option Strategies

B. Maximum Profit

Increase in Stock Price

If stock is above call option striking price at expiration, call options will be exercised.

(11) Sell __200__ shares of __Boeing__ @ __55__ = $ __11,000__
     amount   common   call
     in (1)   stock   strking
                                 price

(12) Less commissions   − __N/A__

(13) Plus dividends received   + __140__

(14) Net proceeds   = $ __11,140__

(15) Profit [(14) − (10)] $ __940__

(16) Return on investment [(15)/(10)]   __9.2__ %

(17) Return annualized [(365)/(days until expiration) × (16)]   __18.45__ %

C. Maximum Risk

If stock falls below put option striking price, put options will be exercised.

(18) Sell __200__ shares of __Boeing__ @ __50__ = $ __10,000__
     amount   common   put
     in (1)   stock   strking
                                 price

(19) Less commissions   − __N/A__

(20) Plus dividends received   + $ __140__

(21) Net proceeds   = $ __10,140__

(22) Potential loss [(10) − (21)] $ __(60)__

(23) Percentage risk [(22)/(10)]   __.588__ %

*You may choose to sell the put options for a profit and continue to hold the stock if you remain bullish.

D. Breakeven at Expiration

If stock is below call striking price and above put striking price, both options will expire worthless, and the average cost per share is:

(24) [(10) − (13) + (commissions to sell stock)/ (no. of shares)]   __50.3__

SYNTHETIC STOCK POSITION

By using put and call options, it is possible for an investor to create a position that is essentially the same as a long stock position, namely a synthetic stock position.

DEFINITION AND LOGIC The *synthetic stock position* offers the same appreciation potential or risk of loss as in the case of purchasing common stock. The major benefit of the synthetic stock position is that it requires less cash than the long stock position. The major shortcoming is that the position is subject to time premium decay. The synthetic stock strategy has the same margin requirements as the short put position discussed in Chapter Four.

The mechanics of the synthetic stock position involve the purchase of a call and the sale of a put with the same striking price and expiration dates. Recall that the short put position *obligates* the investor to purchase the underlying stock at the striking price, while the long call position gives the investor the *right* to purchase the stock at the striking price. Thus, if the stock increases in value and is above the striking price at expiration, the put will expire worthless and the call will appreciate in value. If the stock drops in value to a level below the striking price at expiration, the put will be exercised and the investor will be obligated to purchase the stock at the put option striking price. If the stock is at the striking price at expiration, both the put and the call will expire worthless.

ILLUSTRATION: NATIONAL SEMICONDUCTOR CORPORATION To illustrate the synthetic stock strategy, we will use National Semiconductor Corporation. Suppose that semiconductor sales appear to be improving and you are bullish on the prospects for National Semiconductor. You observe that National Semiconductor common stock is trading at 12½ points and the options are priced as follows:

National Semiconductor 6-month 12½ put, 1½
National Semiconductor 6-month 12½ call, 1½

Since you are bullish on National Semiconductor, you can either purchase 100 shares of stock, or sell one 6-month 12½ put for 1½

Advanced Option Strategies

points and use the premium from the put option to purchase a 6-month 12½ call option. The short put option position creates the obligation to purchase National Semiconductor at 12½, while the long call option position gives you the right to purchase 100 shares of National Semiconductor at 12½.

Following is a comparison of the synthetic stock strategy and the long stock position that should help you appreciate the risks and rewards involved:

Initial Position

National Semiconductor = 12½
June 12 ½ NSM call = 1½
June 12 ½ NSM put = 1½

Stock Position	*Synthetic Stock Position*		
		Debit	*Credit*
Buy 100 NSM @	Sell 1 NSM June 12 ½ put		+150
12½ = $1,200	Buy 1 NSM June 12 ½ call	−150	
	Net investment		0

*Collateral is required for naked put positon

Stock Increases 20% to $15 per share at Expiration:

Profit of 2½	June 12 ½ put exipres worthless	—
points, or $250	Sell June 12 ½ call, which can	
	be sold for 2½ points or	+250
	Gain	+250

Stock Decreases 20% to $10 per share at Expiration:

Loss of 2 ½	June 12 ½ put will be exercised and the stock will
points, or $250	be put to you at $15 per share, resulting a −$250
	loss [12½ (cost of shares) 10 (current price)]

The June 12 ½ call will expire worthless

Stock Stays at $12.50 per share:

No gain or loss	June 12 ½ put will expire worthless
	June 12 ½ call will expire worthless

As you can see, a 20 percent increase in the stock's price will result in a $250 profit for both the long stock position and the synthetic stock position, while a 20 percent decrease will create a $250 loss for both positions.

170   Chapter 7

If you use the synthetic stock strategy, you can avoid having the stock put to you by purchasing a put with the same expiration date and striking price in the options market. If the stock remains at 12½ at expiration, both the put and the call will expire worthless. In this scenario, you will neither profit nor gain. In a situation in which you had a net debit, you would incur a loss equal to the debit.

It is also important to note that the synthetic stock strategy does not pay dividends, which in some cases may improve your total return.

In this example, the put and call premiums are the same. However, this obviously will not always be the case. Worksheet 7-7 will allow you to run through some of your own ideas to see if they are worthwhile. Worksheets 7-8 and 7-9 complete the illustration of the synthetic stock strategy using our National Semiconductor example.

Worksheet 7-7
Synthetic Stock Position

Common stock _____   Current price _____

Put option _____ _____ _____
    month striking premium
        price

Call option _____ _____ _____
    month striking premium
        price

Days until expiration _____

A. Initial Position

	Credit	Debit
(1) Buy _____ calls @ _____ no. premium		$ _____
(2) Plus commissions + _____		
(3) Net debit		$ _____
(4) Sell _____ puts @ _____ no. premium	$ _____	
(5) Less commissions – _____		

Advanced Option Strategies 171

(6) Net credit $ _____

(7) Net position $ _____ $ _____

If there is no change in the stock price, then a loss equal to the amount of the net debt will be incurred.

B. Liquidating Position

Days until expiration _____

(8) Sell _____ calls @ _____ $ _____
   amount   market
   in (1)   price

(9) Less commissions   − $ _____

(10) Net call sale $ _____

(11) Gain (loss) on call position [(10) − (3)] $ _____

(12) Buy _____ puts @ _____ $ _____
   amount   market
   in (4)   price

(13) Plus commissions   + $ _____

(14) Net put purchase $ _____

(15) Gain (loss) on put position $ _____

(16) Net gain (loss) [(7) + (11) + (15)] $ _____

C. Cost Per Share if Put is Exercised

Put options will be exercised if not closed out.

Days until expiration _____

(17) Buy _____ of _____ @ _____ $ _____
  no. of   common   put
  shares   stock   striking
          price

(18) Plus commissions   + $ _____

(19) Minus credit or plus debit in (7)   − $ _____

(20) Net investment $ _____

(21) Average cost per share [(20) divided by number of shares in (17)] $ _____

172   Chapter 7

Worksheet 7-8
Synthetic Stock Position:
National Semiconductor Stock Increase at Expiration

Common stock **National Semiconductor**   Current price **12½**

Put option **June**   **12½**   **1½**
       month   striking premium
                price

Call option **June**   **12½**   **1½**
       month   striking premium
                price

Days until expiration **182**

A. Initial Position

		Credit	Debit
(1) Buy **1** calls @ **1½**			$ **150**
no. premium			
(2) Plus commissions + **N/A**			
(3) Net debit			$ **150**
(4) Sell **1** puts @ **1½**		$ **150**	
no. premium			
(5) Less commissions – **N/A**			
(6) Net credit		$ **150**	
(7) Net position		$ **0**	$ **0**

If there is no change in the stock price, then a loss equal to the amount of the net debit will be incurred.

B. Liquidating Position

Days until expiration **0**

		Debit
(8) Sell **1** calls @ **2½**		$ **250**
amount market in (1) price		
(9) Less commissions	–	$ **N/A**
(10) Net call sale		$ **250**

Advanced Option Strategies 173

(11) Gain (loss) on call position [(10) – (3)] $ __250__

(12) Buy _____ puts @ _____ $ _____
        amount   market
        in (4)   price

(13) Plus commissions   + $ _____

(14) Net put purchase $ _____

(15) Gain (loss) on put position $ _____

(16) Net gain (loss) [(7) + (11) + (15)] $ __250__

C.   Cost Per Share if Put is Exercised

Put options will be exercised if not closed out.

Days until expiration _____

(17) Buy _____ of _____ @ _____ $ _____
        no. of   common   put
        shares   stock   striking
                       price

(18) Plus commissions   + _____

(19) Minus credit or plus debit in (7)   – $ _____

(20) Net investment $ _____

(21) Average cost per share [(20) divided by
     number of shares in (17)] $ _____

Worksheet 7-9
Synthetic Stock Position:
National Semiconductor Stock Decrease at Expiration

Common stock __National Semiconductor__   Current price __12½__

Put option __June__ __12½__ __1½__
        month   striking   premium
                price

Call option __June__ __12½__ __1½__
        month   striking   premium
                price

Days until expiration __182__

A. Initial Position

	Credit	Debit
(1) Buy __1__ calls @ __1½__ 　　　no.　　　　premium		$ __150__
(2) Plus commissions + __N/A__		
(3) Net debit		$ __150__
(4) Sell __1__ puts @ __1½__ 　　　no.　　　　premium	$ __150__	
(5) Less commissions – __N/A__		
(6) Net credit	$ __150__	
(7) Net position	$ __0__	$ __0__

If there is no change in the stock price, then a loss equal to the amount of the net debit will be incurred.

B. Liquidating Position

Days until expiration _____

(8) Sell _____ calls @ _____　　　　　　　　　　$ _____
　　　　　amount　　　market
　　　　　in (1)　　　　price

(9) Less commissions　　　　　　　　　　　　　　　–　$ _____

(10) Net call sale　　　　　　　　　　　　　　　　　　$ _____

(11) Gain (loss) on call position [(10) – (3)]　　　　$ _____

(12) Buy _____ puts @ _____　　　　　　　　　$ _____
　　　　　amount　　　market
　　　　　in (4)　　　　price

(13) Plus commissions　　　　　　　　　　　　　　　+　$ _____

(14) Net put purchase　　　　　　　　　　　　　　　　$ _____

(15) Gain (loss) on put position　　　　　　　　　　　$ _____

(16) Net gain (loss) [(7) + (11) + (15)]　　　　　　　$ _____

C. Cost Per Share if Put is Exercised

Put options will be exercised if not closed out.

Days until expiration __0__

Advanced Option Strategies

(17) Buy	**100**	of	**National Semiconductor** @	**12½**	$	**1,250**
	no. of shares		common stock	put striking price		

(18) Plus commissions	+	**N/A**
(19) Minus credit or plus debit in (7)	– $	**0**
(20) Net investment	$	**1,250**
(21) Average cost per share [(20) divided by number of shares in (17)]	$	**$12.50**

REPAIR STRATEGY

DEFINITION AND LOGIC An investor uses a *repair strategy* to lower the breakeven point in a long stock position that is not working with his or her original investment objective.

ILLUSTRATION: GILLETTE CORPORATION Suppose you purchased 100 shares of Gillette at $62 a share because of takeover rumors. Just a few weeks later, the takeover has not materialized and the stock has fallen to $50 a share.

Now you face a dilemma. Although you still remain bullish on the long-term outlook for Gillette, it would take a 24 percent increase in the value of the stock just for you to break even. As long as you are still bullish on Gillette, there is one strategy you can employ to lower your breakeven point on the stock. First, let's review the current call options available on Gillette. They are priced as follows:

Gillette 6-month 50 call, 5
Gillette 6-month 60 call, 2½

The first step in your repair strategy is to purchase one Gillette 6-month 50 call for 5 points, or $500. Next, you sell two 6-month 60 calls for 2½ points, or $250, each. Your new position will look as follows:

Long 100 shares Gillette
Short one 6-month 60 call } Covered call

Long one 6-month 50 call
Short one 6-month 60 call } Bull spread

As you can see, you have now created a covered call and a bull spread without paying out any more money except for commissions.

The proceeds from the 6-month 60 calls offset the debit for the 6-month 50 call. As discussed in previous chapters, the two short calls are covered because of one long stock position and one long call option position. In some situations, an additional debit is created, and as an investor you have to decide whether or not you want to contribute more to this investment.

Now let's look at some possible results from your new position. Suppose Gillette rebounds to 56, or 12 percent, by expiration. In that case, you will have a 6-point, or $600, loss on your original 100 shares. However, you will have a 6-point, or $600, gain on your bull spread. You may now sell the 50 call for 6 points, while the two short 60 calls will expire worthless. Thus, you will have lowered your breakeven point on Gillette from 62 to 56.

If the stock rises to 61, you will have an $800 profit as opposed to a $200 loss had you done nothing. You can sell the long call of the bull spread for 11 points, or $1,100, and close out the short position by paying $100. Thus, you will net out $1,000 on the bull spread position. The stock will be called away at $60 a share, resulting in a 2-point, or $200, loss on the original stock position. Thus, your net profit will be $800 versus a $100 loss had you done nothing. The point to keep in mind is that you will have recouped a 12-point loss on a 6-point move.

To summarize, an investor has little to lose by using the repair strategy on a currently losing stock position. If the stock rallies at all, the investor will recoup his or her loss much more quickly than by doing nothing. If the stock continues to drop, the investor will lose commission dollars plus any debit incurred. The only situation in which the investor would be better off not employing this strategy is when the stock rallies sharply over a very short time period.

Worksheet 7-9 will help you in creating your own repair strategies. Worksheet 7-10 fills in the data from our Gillette example.

Advanced Option Strategies   177

Worksheet 7-10
Stock Repair Strategy

(1) Common stock _____

(2) Original price paid _____

(3) Current price _____

(4) Call option   _____   _____   _____
    (lower striking price)   month   striking   premium
                                      price

(5) Call option   _____   _____   _____
    (higher striking price)   month   striking   premium
                                      price

A. Initial Position

(6) You had bought _____ of _____ @ _____ = $ _____
                          no. of   common   price
                          shares   stock

(7) Plus commissions   + _____

(8) Net original position   = $ _____

(9) Net cost per share [(6/(no of shares purchased)] $ _____

B. Repair Position

(10) Original posiiton (8) $ _____

(11) Buy _____ _____ _____ _____   + _____
        call (4)   month   striking   premium
                             price

           Amount (1 per 100 Shares of Stock Owned)

(12) Sell _____ _____ _____ _____   − _____
        call (5)   month   strike   premium
                        price

           Amount (to offset Stock and Call Option)

(13) Net commissions for options   − _____

(14) Net cost of repair [(11) − (12) net in (13)]   = $ _____

New positions

Long original shares of stock
Short higher or out-of-the-money call } Covered call

Long lower striking price call
Short higher striking price call } Bull spread

C. Amount Recovered by Repair Strategy
Increase in Stock Price

If stock is above call option with higher striking price at liquidation:

(15) Sell _____ shares of _____ @ _____   = $ _____
      amount   common   higher
      in (6)   stock   call
                                     striking
                                       price

(16) Less commissions   − _____

(17) Plus dividends received   + $ _____

(18) Net proceeds from covered write   = $ _____

(19) Sell (11) position at market price $ _____

(20) Less commissions   − _____

(21) Net proceeds from lower striking
      price call option   = $ _____

(22) Purchase ½ of (12) position $ _____

(23) Plus commissions   + _____

(24) Net cost to close short call position   = $ _____

(25) Profit/loss on original stock position [(18) − (8)] $ _____

(26) Profit from bull spread [(21)+(24)]   + $ _____

(27) Net profit/loss [(25) + (26) − (14)] $ _____

If stock is between the strike prices at liquidation:

(28) Current value of stock $ _____

(29) Dividends received $ _____

(30) Original stock position (8) $ _____

(31) Sell (11) position at market price $ _____

Advanced Option Strategies 179

(32) Less commissions — _____

(33) Net proceeds from lower striking price call option = $ _____

(34) Buy (12) position at market price $ _____

(35) Plus commissions + _____

(36) Net cost to close short call position = $ _____

(37) Change in original stock position value
    [(28) + (29) − (30) + (33) − (36)] $ _____

Worksheet 7-11
Stock Repair Strategy:
Gillette Corporation

(1) Common stock ___**Gillette**___

(2) Original price paid ___**62**___

(3) Current price ___**52**___

(4) Call option   __**June**__   __**50**__   __**5**__
    (lower striking price)   month   striking   premium
                         price

(5) Call option   __**June**__   __**60**__   __**2½**__
    (higher striking price)   month   striking   premium
                         price

A. Initial Position

(6) You had bought ___**100**___ of ___**Gillette**___ @ ___**62**___ = $ ___**6,200**___
                 no. of   common   price
                 shares   stock

(7) Plus commissions + ___**N/A**___

(8) Net original position = $ ___**6,200**___

(9) Net cost per share [(6/(no of shares purchased)] $ ___**62**___

B. Repair Position

(10) Original posiiton (8) $ ___**6,200**___

(11) Buy __1__ __June__ __50__ __5__   + __500__ -

     call (4)   month   striking   premium

                      price

Amount (1 per 100 Shares of Stock Owned)

(12) Sell __2__ __June__ __60__ __2½__   − __500__

     call (5)   month   stike price   premium

Amount (to offset Stock and Call Option)

(13) Net commissions for options   − __N/A__

(14) Net cost of repair [(11) − (12) net in (13)]   = $ __0__

New positions

Long original shares of stock
Short higher or out-of-the-money call } Covered call

Long lower striking price call
Short higher striking price call } Bull spread

C.   Amount Recovered by Repair Strategy
Increase in Stock Price

If stock is above call option with higher striking price at liquidation:

(15) Sell __100__ shares of __Gillette__ @ __60__   = $ __6,000__

     amount   common   higher

     in (6)   stock   call

                                   strking

                                   price

(16) Less commissions   − __N/A__

(17) Plus dividends received   + $ __68__

(18) Net proceeds from covered write   = $ __6,068__

(19) Sell (11) position at market price $ __1,100__

(20) Less commissions   − __N/A__

(21) Net proceeds from lower striking
       price call option   = $ __1,100__

(22) Purchase ½ of (12) position $ __(100)__

(23) Plus commissions   + __N/A__

(24) Net cost to close short call position   = $ __(100)__

(25) Profit/loss on original stock position [((18) − (8)] $ __(132)__

Advanced Option Strategies

(26) Profit from bull spread [(21)+(24)]   + $ __1,000__

(27) Net profit/loss [(25) + (26) − (14)] $ __868__

If stock is between the strike prices at liquidation:

(28) Current value of stock $ _____

(29) Dividends received $ _____

(30) Original stock position (8) $ _____

(31) Sell (11) position at market price $ _____

(32) Less commissions   − _____

(33) Net proceeds from lower striking price call option   = $ _____

(34) Buy (12) position at market price $ _____

(35) Plus commissions   + _____

(36) Net cost to close short call position   = $ _____

(37) Change in original stock position value
     [(28) + (29) − (30) + (33) − (36)] $ _____

CONCLUSION

In this chapter, we built on the fundamental options strategies to help us achieve a variety of investment objectives. If you use your imagination and are proficient in the fundamentals covered in Chapters One through Six, there are an infinite number of options strategies that you can use to better achieve your investment objectives.

PROBLEMS

See Appendix D for solutions.

PROBLEM 7-1

Suppose that on December 1 Boeing Corporation's common stock is at 51 and the 70-day Boeing February 50 put options have a price of 1¾. Since you are bullish on Boeing's long-term prospects, you simultaneously buy 200 shares of Boeing common stock and sell two February 50 put options. In February, one day after the put options' expiration date, Boeing's common stock is at 49 and the February 50 put option is exercised. Compute your cost basis for all 400 shares of Boeing common stock.

PROBLEM 7-2

Suppose that in January Walt Disney Corporation's common stock is at 43, the 75-day Disney March 45 call options are priced at 2¾, and the 75-day Disney March 40 put options have a price of 1½. Since you feel that Disney will either stay stagnant or increase modestly over the next few months, you employ the covered combination strategy. You do this by purchasing 200 shares of Disney common stock for 43 and simultaneously selling two March 45 call options and two March 40 put options. In March, one day after the options' expiration date, Disney common stock is at 48 and the March 45 call option is exercised. Assuming that you have received one quarterly dividend of $.08 per share, compute the annualized return on your investment.

PROBLEM 7-3

Suppose that in April PepsiCo's common is at 27, the 120-day PepsiCo August 30 call options have a price of 1¼, and the 120-day PepsiCo August 25 put options are valued at 1. Since you are bullish on PepsiCo's near-term prospects but concerned about a correction in the stock market, you employ a hedged covered call

Advanced Option Strategies   183

strategy. You do this by purchasing 400 shares of PepsiCo common stock for 27 and simultaneously selling four August 30 call options and buying four August 25 put options. Assuming that you receive two quarterly dividends of $.16 a share, compute your breakeven point, maximum profit, and maximum risk.

PROBLEM 7-4

Suppose that on December 1 the 120-day Avon Products April 30 call option has a price of 2, the 120-day Avon April 30 put option is priced at 1¾, and the price of Avon common stock is 30. Since you feel that Avon's common stock price will increase during the next 120 days, you decide to create a synthetic stock position. You establish this by purchasing an April 30 call option and selling an April 30 put option. In late March, 20 days prior to the options' expiration, the securities are priced as follows:

Avon common stock, 36
Avon April 30 call, 6⅜
Avon April 30 put, ¼

Compute the profit generated by the synthetic stock position if liquidated 20 days prior to the April expiration date.

PROBLEM 7-5

Suppose you purchased 100 shares of General Motors common stock at 85 in April. It is now November, and GM common stock is at 70, the 120-day March 70 call options have a price of 3½, and the 120-day March 75 call options are priced at 1¾. Suggest a repair strategy that you may use to lower your breakeven point on General Motors. Given the new position, calculate your net profit or loss if one month prior to expiration GM common stock is at 78, the March 70 call options are priced at 8½, and the March 75 call options are at 3½. Assume that you have received three quarterly dividends of $1.25 a share.

Appendix
A

BIBLIOGRAPHY

Bookstaber, Richard M. *Option Pricing and Strategies in Investing.* Chicago: Probus, 1987.

Cox, John C., and Mark Rubenstein. *Options Markets.* Englewood Cliffs, NJ: Prentice-Hall, 1985.

Engel, Louis, and Brendon Boyd. *How to Buy Stocks.* Boston: Bantam, 1982.

Hirt, Geoffrey, with Stanley Block and Fred Jury. *The Investor's Desktop Portfolio Planner.* Chicago: Probus, 1986.

Malkiel, Burton G. *A Random Walk Down Wall Street.* New York: Norton, 1980.

McMillan, Lawrence G. *Options as a Strategic Investment.* New York: New York Institute of Finance, 1986.

Appendix
B

Appendix B

GLOSSARY

AT-THE MONEY—A condition in which an underlying stock is trading at the option's striking (exercise) price.

AVERAGE DOWN—A strategy used to lower the average cost of a stock by purchasing more shares at a lower price.

BEAR SPREAD (PUT)—The simultaneous purchase of a put option with a higher striking price and sale of a put option with a lower striking price.

BEARISH—Describes the belief that the market or an individual stock will fall in value.

BULL SPREAD (CALL)—The simultaneous purchase of a call option with a lower striking price and sale of a call option with a higher striking price.

BULLISH—Describes the belief that the market or an individual stock will rise in value.

CALENDAR SPREAD—*See* Time Spread.

CALL OPTION—A contract that gives the purchaser the right to buy a stock at a predetermined price and obligates the seller to deliver the stock at a predetermined price.

COVERED CALL WRITE—A bullish strategy that involves the purchase of common stock while simultaneously selling an equal amount of call options.

COVERED COMBINATION—A bullish strategy in which an investor purchases a stock and simultaneously buys an equal amount of calls and sells an equal amount of puts with different strike prices or expiration dates.

COVERED OPTION—A written option position that has a corresponding stock or option position.

DELTA—A measurement of how much an option price will move relative to the movement of the underlying stock's price. Call options have positive deltas (between 0 and 1); put options have negative deltas (between 0 and −1).

EXERCISE—To use the rights available in an options contract, i.e., to buy the underlying stock (call option) or sell the underlying stock (put option) at the striking price.

EXERCISE PRICE—*See* Striking Price.

FUNDAMENTAL ANALYSIS—A type of analysis that attempts to assess a security's potential by examining data such as sales, earnings, balance sheets, income statements, debt, assets, management, and products.

GOOD TILL CANCELLED (GTC)—An order to buy or sell a security that remains in effect until it is executed (or cancelled).

HEDGE—An offsetting position used to limit risk or loss.

IN-THE-MONEY—With a call option, the condition where the stock's current market price is above the striking price; with a put option, the condition where the stock's current market price is below the striking price.

Glossary 193

INTRINSIC VALUE—For an in-the-money option, the difference between the striking price and the stock's current market value. (Out-of-the-money options have no intrinsic value.) For call options, intrinsic value = stock price – striking price; for put options, intrinsic value = striking price – stock price.

LIMIT ORDER—An order placed with a broker to buy or sell a security at a specified or better price.

LONG POSITION—Ownership of a stock or an opening buy transaction on an option position.

MARGIN ACCOUNT—A brokerage account set up to allow an investor to borrow money for the purchase of securities or securities loaned for short stock sales. Minimum margin requirements may consist of depositing cash or certain marginable securities. These accounts are governed by Regulation T of the Federal Reserve System.

MARKET ORDER—An order to buy or sell a security at the best current market price.

NEUTRAL POSITION—A position that will perform well if the underlying security undergoes little or no change.

OPTIONS CLEARING CORPORATION (OCC)—A corporation that is owned in equal proportions by the option exchanges. It handles all option transactions and guarantees the fulfillment of all rights and obligations involved in a trade. Also issues a prospectus explaining the risks, rules, and ethical standards concerning option accounts.

OUT-OF-THE-MONEY—With a call option, the condition in which the stock's current market price is below the striking price; with a put option, the condition in which the stock's current market price is above the striking price.

PARITY—A condition where the option premium is equal to its intrinsic value (i.e., time value is not a factor).

PREMIUM—The price paid for an option that is equal to the sum of the option's intrinsic value and time value.

PUT OPTION—A contract that gives the purchaser the right to sell a stock at a predetermined price and obligates the seller to purchase the stock at a predetermined price.

RESISTANCE—A term used by technical analysts to describe the price level at which a stock will stop rising or meet resistance based on its previous trading history.

ROLLING DOWN—Simultaneously closing out one option position at a higher striking price and opening another position at a lower striking price.

ROLLING FORWARD—Simultaneously closing out an option position with a near-term expiration date and opening a position with a later expiration date.

ROLLING UP—Simultaneously closing out one position at a lower striking price and opening another position at a higher striking price.

SHORT POSITION—A position that involves selling stock short or an opening sell transaction on an option position.

SHORT STOCK SALE—A bearish strategy in which the initial position is the sale of a security based on the seller's anticipation of a price decline. The investor borrows the security from a broker-dealer at the time of the short sale. If the stock declines, the investor purchases it back at a lower price, thereby gaining a profit. If the stock rises, the investor buys it back at a higher price, thus incurring a loss.

Glossary

STOP-LIMIT ORDER—An order placed with a broker to buy or sell a security at a specified or better price; a combination of a stop order and a limit order.

STOP ORDER—An order placed with a broker to buy or sell a security that is currently trading away from the market. Once the security hits the stop price, the stop order becomes a market order.

STRADDLE—The purchase or sale of an equal number of puts and calls on the same underlying stock with the same striking prices and expiration dates.

STRANGLE—The simultaneous purchase or sale of an equal number of out-of-the-money call and put options.

STRIKING PRICE—The price at which a call option holder may elect to exercise the right to buy the underlying security or a put option holder may choose to exercise the right to sell the underlying security.

SUPPORT LEVEL—A term used by technical analysts to describe the price level at which a stock will stop falling or meet support based on its prior trading history.

SYNTHETIC STOCK POSITION—A bullish option strategy that involves the sale of a put option and the purchase of a call option to obtain the equivalent of ownership of the underlying stock.

TECHNICAL ANALYSIS—A type of analysis that attempts to predict future stock or market price movements by using historical data such as past prices, trading volume, number of advancing shares, and short-selling activity.

TIME SPREAD—The simultaneous sale of a near-term option and purchase of a longer-term option. If the striking prices are the same, it is considered a *horizontal* spread; if different, it is called a *diagonal* spread.

TIME VALUE—The total option premium less the option's intrinsic value.

UNCOVERED (NAKED) OPTION—A written option position that does not have a corresponding position in the underlying stock.

VOLATILITY—The degree to which a security's price rises or falls within a specific time period.

Appendix
C

OPTIONS SOFTWARE

Dollar/Soft
P.O. Box 822-5
Newark, CA 94560
1-415-487-7616

Lotus 1-2-3
Lotus Development Corporation
161 First Street
Cambridge, MA 02142

OPA Software
P.O. Box 90658
Los Angeles, CA 90009
1-800-321-4100

Option Vue Plus
Option Software International
175 E. Hawthorn Parkway
Suite 180
Vernon Hills, IL 60061
312-816-6610

Options Mania
(For Lotus Signal Users)
OM Development Corporation
1331 Eighth Street
Berkeley, CA 94710
1-415-524-5525

Appendix
D

Solutions 203

CHAPTER 5 PROBLEM SOLUTIONS

PROBLEM 5-1

BULL SPREAD PURCHASE WORKSHEET

A. Position Data

Underlying stock **Kellogg**   Current price **32**

Days until option expiration **75**

Options' maturity month **March**

Low striking price **30**   High striking price **35**

Low strike option intrinsic value **2**

Low strike option time value **1½**

Low strike option premium **3½**

High strike option intrinsic value **0**

High strike option time value **1⅞**

High strike option premium **1⅞**

B. Initial Position

(1) Sell **1** high strike options @ **1⅞** for $ **187.50**

(2) Less commissions $ **N/A**

(3) Buy **1** low strike options @ **3½** for $ **350.00**

(4) Plus commissions $ **N/A**

(5) Net cost $ **162.50**

C. Position Profit or Loss

The position's maximum loss will equal the net cost (5) and will occur if both the options are out-of-the-money when they expire. Under these conditions, neither option will have any intrinsic value and both will expire worthless.

Stock price at liquidation **42**

Days until option expiration __7__

Options' maturity month __March__

Low striking price __30__ High striking price __35__

Low strike option intrinsic value __12__

Low strike option time value __1/8__

Low strike option premium   __12 1/8__

High strike option intrinsic value __7__

High strike option time value __1/8__

High strike option premium   __7 1/8__

(6) Buy __1__ high strike options @ __7 1/8__ for $ __712.50__

(7) Plus commissions $ __N/A__

(8) Sell __1__ low strike options @ __12 1/8__ for $ __1,212.50__

(9) Less commissions $ __N/A__

(10) Net revenues $ __500.00__

Net profit or loss [(10) − (5)] $ __337.50__

Solutions
205

PROBLEM 5-2

BULL SPREAD ROLL UP WORKSHEET

A. Initial Position Data

Underlying stock **Kellogg**   Current price **32**

Days until option expiration **75**

Options' maturity month **March**

Low striking price **30**   High striking price **35**

Low strike option intrinsic value **2**

Low strike option time value **1½**

Low strike option premium   **3½**

High strike option intrinsic value **0**

High strike option time value **1⅞**

High strike option premium   **1⅞**

(1) Sell **1** high strike options @ **1⅞** for $ **187.50**

(2) Less commissions $ **N/A**

(3) Buy **1** low strike options @ **3½** for $ **350.00**

(4) Plus commissions $ **N/A**

(5) Net cost $ **162.50**

B. Roll-Up Position Data

Underlying stock **Kellogg**   Current price **40**

Days until option expiration **25**

Option premium **11** @ striking price **30**

Option premium **6⅛** @ striking price **35**

Option premium **2** @ striking price **40**

(6) Sell **1** options strike = **30** @ **11** for $ **1,100**

(7) Less commissions $ __N/A__

(8) Buy __2__ options strike = __35__ @ __6⅛__ for $ __1,225.00__

(9) Plus commissons $ __N/A__

(10) Sell __1__ options strike = __40__ @ __2__ for $ __200.00__

(11) Less commissions $ __N/A__

(12) Roll-up cash flow $ __75.00__

(13) Net cash flow [(12) − (5)] $ __(87.50)__

C. Total Position Profit or Loss

Stock price at liquidation __42__

Days until option expiration __7__

Options' maturity month __March__

Low striking price __35__   High striking price __40__

Low strike option intrinsic value __7__

Low strike option time value __⅛__

Low strike option premium __7⅛__

High strike option intrinsic value __2__

High strike option time value __⅛__

High strike option premium __2⅛__

(14) Buy __1__ options strike = __40__ @ __2⅛__ for $ __212.50__

(15) Plus commissions $ __N/A__

(16) Sell __1__ options strike = __35__ @ __7⅛__ for $ __712.50__

(17) Less commissions $ __N/A__

(18) Net revenues $ __500.00__

Net profit or loss [(18) + (13)] $ __412.50__

Solutions   207

PROBLEM 5-3

BEAR SPREAD PURCHASE WORKSHEET

A. Position Data

Underlying stock __GM__ Current price __75__

Days until option expiration __135__

Options' maturity month __November__

Low striking price __70__ High striking price __75__

Low strike option intrinsic value __0__

Low strike option time value __$1\frac{5}{8}$__

Low strike option premium   __$1\frac{5}{8}$__

High strike option intrinsic value __0__

High strike option time value __3__

High strike option premium   __3__

B. Initial Position

(1) Sell __1__ low strike options @ __$1\frac{5}{8}$__ for $ __162.50__

(2) Less commissions $ __N/A__

(3) Buy __1__ high strike options @__3__ for $ __300.00__

(4) Plus commissions $ __N/A__

(5) Net cost $ __137.50__

C. Position Profit or Loss

The position's maximum loss will equal the net cost (5) and will
occur if both the options are out-of-the-money when they
expire. Under these conditions, neither option will have
any intrinsic value and both will expire worthless.

Stock price at liquidation   __69__

Days until option expiration __4__

Options' maturity month **November**

Low striking price _____**70**_____ High striking price _____**75**_____

Low strike option intrinsic value _____**1**_____

Low strike option time value _____**⅛**_____

Low strike option premium _____**1⅛**_____

High stike option intrinsic value _____**6**_____

High strike option time value_____**0**_____

High strike option premium _____**6**_____

(6) Buy _____**1**_____ low strike options @ _____**1⅛**_____ for $ _____**112.50**_____

(7) Plus commissions $ _____**N/A**_____

(8) Sell _____**1**_____ high strike options @ _____**6**_____ for $ _____**600.00**_____

(9) Less commissions $ _____**N/A**_____

(10) Net revenues $ _____**487.50**_____

Net profit or loss [(10) − (5)] $ _____**350.00**_____

Solutions 209

PROBLEM 5-4

BEAR SPREAD ROLL DOWN WORKSHEET

A. Initial Position Data

Underlying stock __**GM**__ Current price __**75**__

Days until option expiration __**135**__

Options' maturity month **November**

Low striking price __**70**__ High striking price __**75**__

Low strike option intrinsic value __**0**__

Low strike option time value __**$1\frac{5}{8}$**__

Low strike option premium __**$1\frac{5}{8}$**__

High strike option intrinsic value __**0**__

High strike option time value __**3**__

High strike option premium __**3**__

(1) Sell __**1**__ low strike options @ __**$1\frac{5}{8}$**__ for $ __**162.50**__

(2) Less commissions $ __**N/A**__

(3) Buy __**1**__ high strike options @ __**3**__ for $ __**300.00**__

(4) Plus commissions $ __**N/A**__

(5) Net cost $ __**137.50**__

B. Roll-Down Position Data

Underlying stock __**GM**__ Current price __**70**__

Days until option expiration __**35**__

Option premium __**$\frac{7}{8}$**__ @ striking price __**65**__

Option premium __**$2\frac{3}{8}$**__ @ striking price __**70**__

Option premium __**$6\frac{1}{4}$**__ @ striking price __**75**__

(6) Sell __**1**__ options strike = __**75**__ @ __**$6\frac{1}{4}$**__ for $ __**625.00**__

(7) Less commissions $ __**N/A**__

210   Appendix D

(8) Buy __2__ options strike = __70__ @ __2⅜__ for $ __475.00__

(9) Plus commissions $ __N/A__

(10) Sell __1__ options strike = __65__ @ __⅞__ for $ __87.50__

(11) Less commissions $ __N/A__

(12) Roll-down cash flow $ __237.50__

(13) Net cash flow [(12) − (5)] $ __100.00__

C. Total Position Profit or Loss

Stock price at liquidation   __69__

Days until option expiration __4__

Options' maturity month **November**

Low striking price __65__   High striking price __70__

Low strike option intrinsic value __0__

Low strike option time value __⅛__

Low strike option premium   __⅛__

High strike option intrinsic value __1__

High strike option time value __¼__

High strike option premium   __1¼__

(14) Buy __1__ options strike = __65__ @ __⅛__ for $ __12.50__

(15) Plus commissions $ __N/A__

(16) Sell __1__ options strike = __70__ @ __1¼__ for $ __125.00__

(17) Less commissions $ __N/A__

(18) Net revenues $ __112.50__

Net profit or loss [(18) + (13)] $ __212.50__

Solutions   211

PROBLEM 5-5

TIME SPREAD PURCHASE WORKSHEET

A. Position Data

Underlying stock __Mobil__ Current price __30__

Days until near-term option expiration __70__

Nearby options' maturity month __Feb__ Striking price __30__

Long-term option maturity month __May__ Striking price __30__

Nearby option intrinsic value __0__

Nearby option time value __2¾__

Nearby option premium   __2¾__

Long-term option intrinsic value __0__

Long-term option time value __4__

Long-term option premium   __4__

B. Initial Position

(1) Sell __1__ nearby options @ __2¾__   for $ __275.00__

(2) Less commissions $ __N/A__

(3) Buy __1__ long-term options @ __4__   for $ __400.00__

(4) Plus commissions $ __N/A__

(5) Net cost $ __125.00__

C. Position Profit or Loss

The position's maximum loss will equal the net cost (5) and will occur if both the nearby and far-term options are either deep-in-the-money or deep-out-of-the-money when the near-term option expires. Under these conditions, both options will have very little time value and will be virtually equal in price.

Stock price at liquidation   __27__

Days until near-term option expiration __5__

Nearby options' maturity month __Feb__ Striking price __30__

Long-term option maturity month __May__ Striking price __30__

Nearby option intrinsic value __0__

Nearby option time value __$\frac{1}{16}$__

Nearby option premium __$\frac{1}{16}$__

Long-term option intrinsic value __0__

Long-term option time value __$2\frac{1}{8}$__

Long-term option premium __$2\frac{1}{8}$__

(6) Buy __1__ nearby options @ __$\frac{1}{16}$__ for $ __6.25__

(7) Plus commissions $ __N/A__

(8) Sell __1__ long-term options @ __$2\frac{1}{8}$__ for $ __212.50__

(9) Plus commissions $ __N/A__

(10) Net revenues $ __206.25__

Net profit or loss [(10) − (5)] $ __81.25__

Solutions

PROBLEM 5-6

TIME SPREAD ROLL FORWARD WORKSHEET

A. Initial Position Data

Underlying stock __Mobil__ Current price __30__

Days until nearby option expiration __70__

Options' striking price __30__

Nearby option''s maturity month **February**

Long-term options' maturity month __May__

Nearby option intrinsic value __0__

Nearby option time value __2¾__

Nearby option premium __2¾__

Long-term option intrinsic value __0__

Long-term option time value __4__

Long-term option premium __4__

  (1) Sell __1__ nearby options @ __2¾__   for $ __275.00__

  (2) Less commissions $ __N/A__

  (3) Buy __1__ long-term options @ __4__   for $ __400.00__

  (4) Plus commissions $ __N/A__

  (5) Net cost $ __125.00__

B. Roll-Forward Position Data

Underlying stock __Mobil__ Current price __27__

Options' striking price __30__

Option premium __¹⁄₁₆__ at maturity @ **February**

Option premium __2⅛__ at maturity @ __May__

Option premium __3¼__ at maturity @ **August**

214   Appendix D

(6) Buy __1__ options maturity = **February** @ $\frac{1}{16}$ for $ __6.25__

(7) Plus commissions $ __N/A__

(8) Sell __2__ options maturity = __May__ @ $2\frac{1}{8}$ for $ __425.00__

(9) Less commissions $ __N/A__

(10) Buy __1__ options maturity = **August** @ $3\frac{1}{4}$ for $ __325.00__

(11) Plus commissions $ __N/A__

(12) Roll-forward cash flow $ __93.75__

(13) Net cash flow [(12) − (5)] $ __(31.25)__

C. Total Position Profit or Loss

Stock price at liquidation   __$30\frac{1}{8}$__

Days until nearby option expires __4__

Options' striking price __30__

Nearby option maturity month __May__

Long-term option maturity month __August__

Nearby option intrinsic value __$\frac{1}{8}$__

Nearby option time value __$\frac{1}{8}$__

Nearby option premium   __$\frac{1}{4}$__

Long-term option intrinsic value __$\frac{1}{8}$__

Long-term option time value __$2\frac{7}{8}$__

Long-term option premium   __3__

(14) Buy __1__ options maturity = __May__ at __$\frac{1}{4}$__ for $ __25.00__

(15) Plus Commissions $ __N/A__

(16) Sell __1__ options maturity = **August** at __3__ for $ __300.00__

(17) Less Commissions $ __N/A__

(18) Net Revenues $ __275.00__

Net profit or loss [(18) + (13)] $ __243.75__

Solutions   215

PROBLEM 6-1

STRADDLE PURCHASE WORKSHEET

A. Position Data

Underlying stock __GTE__   Current price __34⅛__

Days until option expiration __125__

Call option maturity month **September**   Striking price __35__

Put option maturity month **September**   Striking price __35__

Call option intrinsic value __0__

Call option time value __3½__

Call option premium   __3½__

Put option intrinsic value __⅞__

Put option time value __2½__

Put option premium   __3⅜__

B. Initial Position

(1) Buy __1__ calls @ __3½__   for $ __350.00__

(2) Plus commissions $ __N/A__

(3) Buy __1__ put @ __3⅜__   for $ __337.50__

(4) Plus commissions $ __N/A__

(5) Net cost $ __687.50__

C. Position Profit or Loss

The position's maximum loss will equal the net cost (5) and will occur if the stock price equals the options' exercise price at maturity. Under these conditions, both options will expire worthless.

Stock price at liquidation   __40⅛__

Days until option expiration __28__

Call option intrinsic value __5⅛__

Call option time value _____2⅛_____

Call option premium _____7¼_____

Put option intrinsic value _____0_____

Put option time value _____1_____

Put option premium _____1_____

Straddle value $ _____825.00_____

(6) Sell _____1_____ calls @ _____7¼_____ for $ _____725.00_____

(7) Less commissions $ _____N/A_____

(8) Sell _____1_____ puts @ _____1_____ for $ _____100.00_____

(9) Less commissions $ _____N/A_____

(10) Net revenues $ _____825.00_____

Net profit or loss [(10) − (5)] $ _____137.50_____

Solutions   217

PROBLEM 6-2

STRADDLE SALE WORKSHEET

A. Position Data

Underlying stock __**GTE**__   Current price __34⅛__

Days until option expiration __125__

Call options' maturity month **September**   Striking price __35__

Put option maturity month **September**   Striking price __35__

Call option intrinsic value __0__

Call option time value __3½__

Call option premium   __3½__

Put option intrinsic value __⅞__

Put option time value __2½__

Put option premium   __3⅜__

B. Initial position

(1) Sell __1__ calls @ __3½__   for $ __350.00__

(2) Less commissions $ __N/A__

(3) Sell __1__ puts @ __3⅜__   for $ __337.50__

(4) Less commissions $ __N/A__

(5) Net revenues $ __687.50__

C. Position Profit or Loss

The position's maximum loss has no upper limit. Large losses
will occur if the stock's price is much greater than the call
option's exercise price at maturity.

Stock price at liquidation   __40⅛__

Days until option expiration __28__

Call option intrinsic value __5⅛__

Call option time value $2\frac{1}{8}$

Call option premium $7\frac{1}{4}$

Put option intrinsic value 0

Put option time value 1

Put option premium 1

Straddle value 825.00

(6) Buy __1__ calls @ __7¼__   for $ 725.00

(7) Plus commissions $ N/A

(8) Buy __1__ puts @ __1__   for $ 100.00

(9) Plus commissions $ N/A

(10) Net costs   825.00

Net profit or loss [(5) − (10)] $ (137.50)

Solutions 219

PROBLEM 6-3

STRANGLE SALE WORKSHEET

A. Position Data

Underlying stock **Digital Equipment**   Current price __104⅛__

Days until option expiration __108__

Call option maturity month __April__   Striking price __110__

Put option maturity month __April__   Striking price __100__

Call option intrinsic value __0__

Call option time value __8¼__

Call option premium   __8¼__

Put option intrinsic value __0__

Put option time value __6¾__

Put option premium   __6¾__

B. Initial Position

(1) Sell __1__ calls @ __8¼__   for $ __825.00__

(2) Less commissions $ __N/A__

(3) Sell __1__ put @ __6¾__   for $ __675.00__

(4) Less commissions $ __N/A__

(5) Net revenues $ __1,500.00__

C. Position Profit or Loss

The position's maximum loss has no upper limit. Large losses will occur if the stock's price is much greater than the call option's exercise price or much less than the put option's exercise price at maturity.

Stock price at liquidation   __172⅞__

Days until option expiration __28__

Call option intrinsic value __**62⅞**__

Call option time value __**⅛**__

Call option premium   __**63**__

Put option intrinsic value __**0**__

Put option time value __**1/16**__

Put option premium   __**1/16**__

Straddle value $ __**6,306.25**__

(6) Buy __**1**__ calls @ __**63**__   for $ __**6,300**__

(7) Plus commissions $ __**N/A**__

(8) Buy __**1**__ puts @ __**1/16**__   for $ __**6.25**__

(9) Plus commissions $ __**N/A**__

(10) Net costs $ __**6,306.25**__

Net profit or loss [(5) − (10)] $ __**(4,806.25)**__

Solutions   221

PROBLEM 6-4

STRANGLE PURCHASE WORKSHEET

A. Position Data

Underlying stock __**Digital Equipment**__ Current price __**104⅛**__

Days until option expiration __**108**__

Call options' maturity month __**April**__ Striking price __**110**__

Put option maturity month __**April**__ Striking price __**100**__

Call option intrinsic value __**0**__

Call option time value __**8¼**__

Call option premium   __**8¼**__

Put option intrinsic value __**0**__

Put option time value __**6¾**__

Put option premium   __**6¾**__

B. Initial position

(1) Buy __**1**__ calls @ __**8¼**__   for $ __**825.00**__

(2) Plus commissions $ __**N/A**__

(3) Buy __**1**__ put @ __**6¾**__   for $ __**675.00**__

(4) Plus commissions $ __**N/A**__

(5) Net cost $ __**1,500.00**__

C. Position Profit or Loss

The position's maximum loss will equal the net cost (5) and will occur if the stock price is between the options' exercise price at maturity. Under these conditions, both options will expire worthless.

Stock price at liquidation   __**172⅞**__

Days until option expiration __**28**__

Call option intrinsic value __**62⅞**__

Call option time value ___$\frac{1}{8}$___

Call option premium ___63___

Put option intrinsic value ___0___

Put option time value ___$\frac{1}{16}$___

Put option premium ___$\frac{1}{16}$___

Strangle value $ __6,306__

(6) Sell ___1___ calls @ ___63___   for $ __6,300__

(7) Less commissions $ __N/A__

(8) Sell ___1___ puts @ ___$\frac{1}{16}$___   for $ __6.25__

(9) Less commissions $ __N/A__

(10) Net revenues $ __6,306.25__

Net profit or loss [(10) − (5)] $ __4,806.25__

Solutions

223

PROBLEM 7-1

BUYING STOCK AND SELLING PUTS SIMULTANEOUSLY

Common stock **Boeing** Current price ____**51**____

Put option **February** ____**50**____ ____**1¾**____
  month striking premium
       price

Days until expiration ____**70**____

A. Initial Position

(1) Buy ____**200**____ of **Boeing** @ ____**51**____ = $ ____**10,200**____
   no. of   common   price
   shares   stock

(2) Plus commissions + ____**N/A**____

(3) Net stock position $ ____**10,200**____

(4) Sell ____**2**____ puts @ ____**1¾**____ $ ____**350**____
    no.   premium

(5) Less commissions − ____**N/A**____

(6) Net put options proceeds = $ ____**350**____

(7) Net cost of positon [(3) − (6)] $ ____**9,850**____

(8) Net cost per share [(7)/(no. of shares purchased)] $ ____**49.25**____

B. Result of Position If Put Are Exercised
  (Occurs if stock is below striking price)

(9) Buy ____**200**____ of **Boeing** @ ____**50**____ = $ ____**10,000**____
   no. of   stock   put striking
   shares   price

(10) Plus commissions + ____**N/A**____

(11) Cost of shares put to you = $ ____**10,000**____

(12) Cost of original shares purchased (7) + ____**9,850**____

(13) Net cost of total shares = $ ____**19,850**____

(14) Net cost per share [(13)/(no. of shares)] $ ____**49.625**____

If stock is at or above striking price, your cost basis is (8).

---

224   Appendix D

PROBLEM 7-2

SELLING COVERED COMBINATIONS

Common stock **Disney**   Current price ___**43**___

Put option **March**   **40**   **1½**
            month   striking   premium
                         price

Call option **March**   **45**   **2¾**
            month   striking   premium
                         price

Days until expiration ___**75**___

A. Initial Position

(1) Buy ___**200**___ of **Disney** @ ___**43**___   = $ ___**8,600**___
        no. of   common   price
        shares   stock

(2) Plus commissions   +   ___**N/A**___

(3) Net stock position $ ___**8,600**___

(4) Sell ___**2**___ calls @ ___**2¾**___ $ ___**550**___
         no.   premium

(5) Less commissions   –   ___**N/A**___

(6) Net call option proceeds   = $ ___**550**___

(7) Sell ___**2**___ puts @ ___**1½**___ $ ___**300**___
         no.   premium

(8) Less commissions   –   ___**N/A**___

(9) Net put options proceeds   = $ ___**300**___

(10) Net investment [(3) – (6) – (9)] $ ___**7,750**___

B. Maximum Profit

Increase in Stock Price

If stock is above call option striking price at expiration, call options
will be exercised.

Solutions

(11) Sell __200__ shares of __Disney__ @ __45__ = $ __9,000__
　　　　　amount　　　　　common　　　call
　　　　　in (1)　　　　　　stock　　　　striking
　　　　　　　　　　　　　　　　　　　　price

(12) Less commissions　　　　　　　　　　　　– __N/A__

(13) Plus dividends received　　　　　　　　　+ __16__

(14) Net proceeds　　　　　　　　　　　　　$ __9,016__

(15) Profit [(14) – (10)]　　　　　　　　　　$ __1,266__

(16) Return on investment [(15)/(10)]　　　　__16.30__ %

(17) Return annualized [(365)/(days until
　　　expiration) × (16)]　　　　　　　　__79.33__ %

Decrease in Stock Price

If stock is below put option striking price at expiration, put options
will be exercised.

(18) Buy _____ shares of _____ @ _____ = $ _____
　　　　amount　　　　　common　　　put
　　　　in (1)　　　　　　stock　　　strking
　　　　　　　　　　　　　　　　　price

(19) Plus commission　　　　　　　　　　　　+ _____

(20) Net cost of new shares　　　　　　　　= $ _____

(21) Average cost of all shares per share
　　　　[(10) + (20) – (amount of dividends received)/
　　　　(total no. of shares)]　　　　　　　　$ _____

Neutral

If stock is between put and call striking prices at expiration, neither
option will be exercised.

(22) Profit [(current value of shares) + (13) – (10)]　　$ _____

(23) Return on investment [(22)/(10)]　　　　_____ %

(24) Return annualized [(365)/(days until
　　　expiration) × (23)]　　　　　　　　_____ %

226   Appendix D

PROBLEM 7-3

HEDGED COVERED CALL WRITE

Common stock **PepsiCo**   Current price ___27___

Put option **August**   ___25___   ___1___
       month   striking   premium
              price

Call option **August**   ___30___   ___1¼___
      month   striking   premium
             price

Days until expiration ___120___

A.   Initial Position

(1) Buy ___400___ of **PepsiCo** @ ___27___   = $ ___10,800___
      no. of   common   price
      shares   stock

(2) Plus commissions   + ___N/A___

(3) Net stock investment $ ___10,800___

(4) Sell ___4___ calls at ___1¼___ $ ___500___
      no.   premium

(5) Less commissions   − ___N/A___

(6) Net call option proceeds $ ___500___

(7) Buy ___4___ puts at ___1___ $ ___400___
      no.   premium

(8) Plus commissions   + ___N/A___

(9) Net put option investment   = $ ___400___

(10) Net investment [(3) − (6) + (9)] $ ___10,700___

Solutions

B. Maximum Profit

Increase in Stock Price

If stock is above call option striking price at expiration, call options will be exercised.

(11) Sell __400__ shares of **PepsiCo** @ __30__ = $ __12,000__
       amount   common   call
        in (1)   stock   strking
                              price

(12) Less commissions   − __N/A__

(13) Plus dividends received   + __64__

(14) Net proceeds   = $ __12,064__

(15) Profit [(14) − (10)] $ __1,364__

(16) Return on investment [(15)/(10)]   __12.75__ %

(17) Return annualized [(365)/(days until expiration) × (16)]   __38.77__ %

C. Maximum Risk

If stock falls below put option striking price, put options will be exercised.

(18) Sell __400__ shares of **PepsiCo** @ __25__ = $ __10,000__
       amount   common   put
        in (1)   stock   strking
                              price

(19) Less commissions   − __N/A__

(20) Plus dividends received   + $ __64__

(21) Net proceeds   = $ __10,064__

(22) Potential loss [(10) − (21)] $ __636__

(23) Percentage risk [(22)/(10)]   __5.94__ %

*You may choose to sell the put options for a profit and continue to hold the stock if you remain bullish.

D. Breakeven at Expiration

If stock is below call striking price and above put striking price, both options will expire worthless.

(24) [(10) − (13) + (commissions to sell stock)/ (no. of shares)] $ __26.59__

228   Appendix D

PROBLEM 7-4

SYNTHETIC STOCK POSITION

Common stock __Avon__ Current price __30__

Put option __April__ __30__ __1¾__
          month   striking   premium
                    price

Call option __April__ __30__ __2__
           month   striking   premium
                      price

Days until expiration __120__

A. Initial Position

	Credit	Debit
(1) Buy __1__ calls@ __2__ no. premium		$ __200__
(2) Plus commissions + __N/A__		
(3) Net debit	=	$ __200__
(4) Sell __1__ puts @ __1¾__ no. premium	$ __175__	
(5) Less commissions – __N/A__		
(6) Net credit	= $ __175__	
(7) Net positon	$ _____	$ __25__

If there is no change in the stock price, then a loss equal to the amount
of the net debit will be incurred.

B. Liquidating Position

Days until expiration __20__

(8) Sell __1__ calls@ __6⅜__ amount market in (1) price		__637.50__
(9) Less commissions	–	$ __N/A__
(10) Net call sale		$ __637.50__

Solutions

(11) Gain (loss on call position [(10) − (3)] $ __437.50__

(12) Buy __1__ puts @ __¼__ $ __25__
       amount   market
       in (4)   price

(13) Plus commissions   + $ __N/A__

(14) Net put purchase $ __25__

(15) Gain (loss) on put position [(6) − (14)] $ __150__

(16) Net gain (loss) [(7) + (11) + (15)] $ __562.50__

C. Cost Per Share if Put is Exercised
Put options will be exercised if not closed out.

Days until expiration _____

(17) Buy _____ of _____ @ _____ $ _____
       no. of   common   put
       shares   stock   striking
                                price

(18) Plus commissions   + $ _____

(19) Minus credit or plus debit in (7)   − $ _____

(20) Net investment $ _____

(21) Average cost per share [(20) divided
     by number of shares in (17)] $ _____

230   Appendix D

PROBLEM 7-5

STOCK REPAIR STRATEGY

(1) Common stock __General Motors__

(2) Original price paid _____ __85__ _____

(3) Current price _____ __70__ _____

(4) Call option   __March__   __70__   __3½__
     (lower striking price)   month   striking   premium
                                                  price

(5) Call option   __March__   __75__   __1¾__
     (higher striking price)   month   striking   premium
                                                  price

A.   Initial Position

(6) You had bought ___ __100__ ___ of ___ __GM__ ___ @ ___ __85__ ___ = $ ___ __8,500__ ___
                        no. of   common   price
                        shares   stock

(7) Plus commissions   + ___ __N/A__ ___

(8) Net original position   = $ ___ __8,500__ ___

(9) Net cost per share [(6)/(no of shares purchased)] $ ___ __85__ ___

B.   Repair Position

(10) Original posiiton (8) $ ___ __8,500__ ___

(11) Buy ___ __1__ ___   __March__   __70__   __3½__   + ___ __350__ ___
         call (4)   month   striking   premium
                                  price

            Amount (1 per 100 Shares of Stock Owned)

(12) Sell ___ __2__ ___   __March__   __75__   __1¾__   − ___ __350__ ___
          call (5)   month   strike   premium
                                   price

            Amount (to offset Stock and Call Option)

(13) Net commissions for options   − ___ __N/A__ ___

(14) Net cost of repair [(11) − (12) net in (13)]   = $ ___ __0__ ___

Solutions

New positions

Long original shares of stock
Short higher or out-of-the-money call $\Big\}$ Covered call

Long lower striking price call
Short higher striking price call $\Big\}$ Bull spread

C. Amount Recovered by Repair Strategy
Increase in Stock Price

If stock is above call option with higher striking price at liquidation:

(15) Sell __100__ shares of __GM__ @ __75__ = $ __7,500__
     amount   common   higher
     in (6)   stock   call
              strking
              price

(16) Less commissions   – __N/A__

(17) Plus dividends received   + $ __375__

(18) Net proceeds from covered write   = $ __7,875__

(19) Sell (11) position at market price $ __850__

(20) Less commissions   – __N/A__

(21) Net proceeds from lower striking
    price call option   = $ __850__

(22) Purchase ½ of (12) position $ __(350)__

(23) Plus commissions   + __N/A__

(24) Net cost to close short call position   = $ __(350)__

(25) Profit/loss on original stock position [(18) – (8)] $ __(625)__

(26) Profit from bull spread [(21)+(24)]   + $ __500__

(27) Net profit/loss [(25) + (26) – (14)] $ __125__

If stock is between the strike prices at liquidation:

(28) Current value of stock $ _____

(29) Dividends received $ _____

(30) Original stock position (8) $ _____

(31) Sell (11) position at market price $ _____

(32) Less commissions   – _____

(33) Net proceeds from lower striking price call
option   = $ _____

(34) Buy (12) position at market price $ _____

(35) Plus commissions   + _____

(36) Net cost to close short call position   = $ _____

(37) Change in original stock position value
[(28) + (29) – (30) + (33) – (36)] $ _____

Appendix
E

ABOUT THE AUTHORS

CARL F. LUFT is an assistant professor of finance at De Paul University. He earned an M.B.A. in international business from De Paul in 1977 and a Ph.D. in finance from Georgia State University in 1983. While completing his doctoral degree, Mr. Luft served as a consultant with the Atlanta branch of Cantor-Fitzgerald Brokerage House. Since returning to Chicago, he has consulted with Cargill Investor Services and taught at the Chicago Board Options Exchange's Options Institute, and the Chicago Mercantile Exchange.

RICHARD K. SHEINER is an investment broker and a registered Options Principal with a leading investment banking firm headquartered in Chicago. He advises individuals and corporations on investment portfolios of stocks, bonds, and options. Mr. Sheiner has been qualified by the Board of Options Institute to teach option investment strategies to both clients and fellow investment professionals. He occasionally conducts courses in options and investments in the Chicago metropolitan area. Mr. Sheiner is a graduate of The University of Michigan, where his studies emphasized business and psychology.